D0933668

The Plains Apache

John Upton Terrell is a leading scholar and historian of the earliest people to inhabit the United States. His many books include *Apache Chronicle*, *The Navajo*, and *Estevanico the Black*. He resides in California.

Books By
JOHN UPTON TERRELL

The Plains Apache
Indian Women of the Western Morning
(with Donna M. Terrell)
Pueblos, Gods and Spaniards
Apache Chronicle
American Indian Almanac
The Man Who Rediscovered America
Traders of the Western Morning
Journey Into Darkness
Zebulon Pike
Estevanico the Black
Faint the Trumpet Sounds
Pueblo de los Corazones
Sunday Is the Day You Rest
Land Grab
Bunkhouse Papers
The Navajo
La Salle
The Six Turnings
Black Robe
Furs By Astor
War for the Colorado River
Plume Rouge
Adam Cargo
The Little Dark Man

THE PLAINS APACHE

by John Upton Terrell

THOMAS Y. CROWELL COMPANY
New York   Established 1834

The publisher thanks the following for permission to use
quotations: the University of New Mexico Press, for material
from George P. Hammond and Agapito Rey, *Don Juan De
Oñate, Colonizer of New Mexico, 1595–1638*, copyright © 1953
by University of New Mexico Press, and from Hammond and
Rey, *The Rediscovery of New Mexico*, copyright © 1966 by
University of New Mexico Press; the University of Oklahoma
Press, for material from George Hyde, *Indians of the High
Plains*, and from Alfred Barnaby Thomas, *After Coronado*.

Designed by Ingrid Beckman
Manufactured in the United States of America

Library of Congress Cataloging in Publication Data

Terrell, John Upton, 1900–
    The Plains Apache.

    Bibliography: p.
    Includes index.
    1. Apache Indians. I. Title.
E99.A6T42   978'.004'97   75-9601
ISBN 0-690-00969-0
10 9 8 7 6 5 4 3 2 1

To My Good Friend
GUTHRIE R. PRICE, M.D.

Author's Note

In my research I have not found another work devoted entirely to the Plains Apache. The reason for this omission escapes me, for they long occupied a position of great importance in western history.

They comprised an immense division of one of the largest linguistic families in the territory of the United States. Their culture was the prototype of the way of life adopted by several other peoples who, emerging from woodlands of the American Middle West and arid tramontane regions, became Indians of the Great Plains. Among them were Siouan, Shoshonean, and Caddoan tribes. The chronicles of the earliest Spanish explorations in New Mexico, Texas, Oklahoma, Colorado, Kansas, and Nebraska tell in considerable detail of encounters—some of them peaceable, and some of them bloody and disastrous—with the Plains Apache.

This narrative represents a conscientious effort to portray the Plains Apache as they appeared, and as they lived and died, in their traditional homeland, the High Plains that break against the southernmost barriers of the Rocky Mountains.

—JOHN UPTON TERRELL

Contents

Maps

PART ONE

The Long Trail

1

In the autumn of 1535, three Spaniards and a Negro Moor, followed by a throng of curious Indians, were pushing westward on foot across the vast plateau of western Texas. Somewhere in this rough, arid land—perhaps not a great distance north of the present town of San Angelo—the four men came upon a camp of some people who were obviously nomads, who spoke a tongue completely different from any they previously had heard, and whose faces and bodies were painted in a variety of intricate patterns with which they were unfamiliar.

This occurrence presaged no significant consequences, but in time it would prove to be of exceeding importance in the historical record of the Plains Apache.

The three white men, all former officers of the Spanish army, were Álvar Núñez Cabeza de Vaca, Andrés Dorantes de Carranco, and Alonso del Castillo Maldonado. The black man, a slave owned by Dorantes, was called Estevanico, and if he had another name, it has not been preserved.

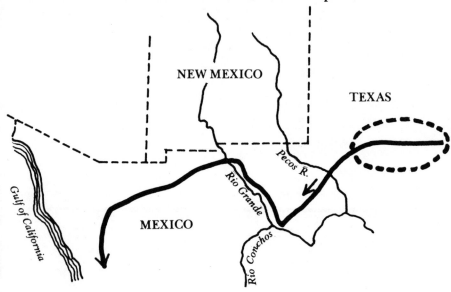

Núñez Cabeza de Vaca and Three Companions

NEW MEXICO

TEXAS

Pecos R.

Rio Grande

Gulf of California

MEXICO

Rio Conchos

⟶ Approximate route

- - - - First men of the Old World to meet Plains
Apache. Discovered them in this area
in 1535

Scale: 1 inch is approximately 200 miles

They were the only survivors of the large expedition of Pánfilo de Narváez which, in the spring of 1528, had set out overland from an arm of Tampa Bay to search for treasure in the unexplored swamps and forests that reached away an unknown distance to the north. In northern Florida a number of men—soldiers, gentleman adventurers, and priests—had been slain in fights with Indians, and others had died of malnutrition, fever, and dysentery.

In a desperate attempt to save themselves, the remaining members of the company, many of them wounded or ill, had constructed five makeshift barges and had sailed westward along the northern coast of the Gulf of Mexico. Totally ignorant of the geography of the region, they had mistakenly concluded that instead of their starting place near Tampa Bay (where ships were still awaiting their return) the closest haven of salvation was Pánuco, a small slaving port in Mexico.

The fragile, unseaworthy craft had been destroyed in a November storm at various places on the Texas coast below Galveston.[1] Almost six years later, out of more than two hundred men suffering this disaster, only Núñez Cabeza de Vaca, Dorantes, Castillo, and Estevanico were still living. During most of this period they had been held captive and forced to labor as slaves. Having traveled with the Indians holding them through extensive areas of the Texas coastal plain, they had become convinced that an attempt to flee southward would end in their being recaptured, and that their only chance of gaining freedom lay in striking out blindly toward the west, praying that they would be able to find some Spanish settlement on the South Sea (the Pacific Ocean). They had no knowledge of the immense distance then between them and the Pacific. For them it would be a journey into complete geographical darkness.

They had pledged themselves to remain together as long as possible. At last, late in September 1534, they had been able to slip away from their captors. It had taken them another year to reach western Texas.

By this time they had passed through territories occupied by thousands of Indians. Coming upon some whose customs, personal adornments, and language differed from those of others they had encountered was a commonplace experience. Moreover, it seems apparent that nothing happened or was learned during their meeting with the strange native wanderers on the western Texas plateau to impress the occasion indelibly on their memories. In all probability they soon forgot about it.

But that was not true of the nomads. If, through the long channels of intertribal trade, or by some other means of wilderness communication, they had heard rumors that men who were white and some who were black had appeared mysteriously out of the eastern sea, it is certain that they had never seen one of either race. And there was another good reason why the nomads would remember the event: the leader of the four men (Núñez Cabeza de Vaca) had told them by signs of an all-powerful deity who ruled the world from the sky; he had counseled them to live in peace with each other; and he had made the sign of a peculiar cross over them and all their possessions.

Then, as unceremoniously as they had appeared, the three bearded white men and the black man, followed by the peaceful Indian men, women, and children who had come with them, had gone on, vanishing into the west.[2]

Six years later, in the late summer of 1541, an advance contingent of the expedition of Francisco Vásquez de Coronado filed on their fine horses down into a deep barranca —perhaps Tule Canyon—in the Texas Panhandle. Camped there was a large band of Indians who *lived like Arabs*.

In the course of a council, an aged man, whose sight was failing, transmitted by signs some information that startled the Spaniards. On a day long past, far to the south, he told

them, he and his people had seen three white men and a
black man.

Thus, in the written accounts of the Coronado Expedition, it would be certified that Núñez Cabeza de Vaca, Dorantes, Castillo, and Estevanico were the first men of the Old
World to meet the Plains Apache.

2

Begin with a name: *Apache*. It did not come, not even by white man's corruption, from the language of the Indians who would bear it in written history. Their name for themselves was *Indé*, meaning "the people." Some branches employed dialectical variations, such as *Tindé* and *N'de* and *Dǐnë*, the latter being the form used by the tribe that would become better known to the world as the Navajo.

Apache was twisted by Spanish tongues from *apachu*, a word with which the Zuni, speaking their own distinct language, designated the *Dǐnë*. *Apachu* signified "enemy." When, in time, the Spanish came to know that the *Indé* and the *Dǐnë* were consanguineous, they called both of them *Apache*, that is, their "enemies," and they had very good reasons for choosing the term. Don Juan de Oñate, the brutish colonizer of the province of New Mexico, may have been the first Spanish authority to give the name official recognition. It appeared in a communication sent by him to the Viceroy of Mexico in 1598, and he was applying it to the Apache of the Plains.

Begin with a trail twisting away from the eastern shore of

the Bering Strait, the shallow, narrow water-passage that
separates North America from Asia. The first human foot-
prints on it were made far back in the Pleistocene, the latest
of the great geological epochs, sometimes referred to as the
Ice Age. That was the start of the trail on this continent.
But it had been much longer, for there was not always the
barrier of icy water between the two land masses. It has
been indisputably proven by scientists that the bottom of
the Bering Strait was exposed for a long period of time. On
this land bridge both people and animals crossed from Siberia to Alaska.

The Bering Strait is shallow. If the water level were to
fall only one hundred and twenty feet even today, the Strait
would not be there. Once more a land bridge would exist
between the two continents. Moreover, it is only fifty-six
miles in width, and this distance is broken by islands. The
widest expanse of open sea is only twenty-five miles. The
land bridge of the Pleistocene would have provided natural
fodder for grazing animals.

All of northern North America was never covered by ice
at the same time. Through countless millennia, as clima-
tological metamorphoses occurred, glaciers advanced and
retreated, reaching deep into the continent and withdrawing. Important as far as the migrants from Asia are concerned is the geological knowledge that for long periods
there were ice-free corridors through which both men and
animals could have passed. That they had traveled as far
south as the region of the United States long before the end
of the Ice Age can no longer be questioned, for evidence
of their presence at least forty thousand years ago has been
discovered. The center of the last major glacial period of
some twenty-five thousand years ago was in the vicinity of
Hudson Bay. Far to the west there was considerably less ice,
and there were ice-free passages opening the way to the
south. Long before that time, however, periods called inter-

stadials during which men and animals would not have been confronted with impassable ice barriers, had occurred in various northern regions.

When the ancestors of the Plains Apache first reached North America, and when they first saw the Great Plains of the southwest that would become their historical homeland, probably can never be finally determined. Certainly they did not originate in any part of the New World. Man evolved from brute ancestry in the Old World and reached North America as a member of the single modern species called *Homo sapiens*, "wise man." His nearest animal relatives, the anthropoid apes, are all found in the Old World. There is a total absence in the New World of missing links and other intermediate fossil forms in man's family tree. In the Old World paleontologists have found hundreds of skeletons of persons intermediate in physical type between men and apes.

The Apache are Mongoloids, as are all other peoples of North America who were erroneously called "Indians" by Columbus.

But if it cannot be stated on the basis of evidence exactly when the Plains Apache crossed the Bering Strait land bridge, neither can it be contended that they were not among the earliest Asiatic migrants. Men hunted the great animals of the Pleistocene in the United States region. Flaked and grooved stone spear points have been found embedded in the bones of Ice Age mammals, the giant bison, the mammoth, the camel, and other species, that were extinct many thousands of years before Norsemen sighted the rocky green shores of Canada or New England.

There is nothing to prove that the people of the earliest cultures of the High Plains were not forebears of the people who in the sixteenth century A.D. would be given the name "Plains Apache." Nor is there anything to support the postulation of some archaeologists that the Plains Apache (and the Navajo) were newcomers, or late arrivals, in the southwest, that they did not reach it until a few centuries prior to the beginning of the historical period. What the scholars who advance this opinion are really saying is that artifacts have not been discovered to show conclusively that the Plains Apache began to infiltrate the High Plains abutting the southern Rocky Mountains prior to the latter centuries of the first millennium of the Christian Era. That is true, but, the absence of material evidence is not acceptable as confirmation that they were not present in the region at a much earlier time. Primitive hunting people, continually drifting in their search for sustenance, would not leave telltale markings to delineate their wanderings.

Although it is not possible to construct a chronology that suggests even approximately when the Plains Apache started their long journey or when they ended it where Europeans found them, their language clarifies unmistakably certain matters reflecting on their remote past.

In prehistoric times, the Athapascan linguistic family, to which the Plains Apache belong, was more widely distributed than any other in North America. People speaking this tongue created what may be termed "inland islands of Athapascans," separated by hundreds, and in some cases by thousands, of miles, from the valleys of the Yukon River and its tributaries to the delta of the Rio Grande, from the American Pacific Coast to the Great Plains.

More than a score of tribes of Athapascan stock, some with several subdivisions, still dwell in Alaska and northwestern Canada, and it is believed that after crossing the Bering Strait from Siberia—a very long time ago—they spread out in this vast territory. Its climate, its animals, and other natural resources were very little different, if at all, from those of the part of Asia they had put behind them. They chose to go no farther.

But, obviously, not all Athapascans were satisfied to

remain in the far northern regions. They trickled on southward, undoubtedly advancing very slowly, in small bands
over a great period of time, for they were entirely depend-
ent upon game and wild plant foods and could not move
rapidly or in large numbers. Geography, geology, paleo-
botany, archaeology, paleontology, and ethnology, each in
its own peculiar way provides clues to the routes they took.

Two main avenues of travel were open to all peoples
from the north. One was along, or adjacent to, the Pacific
Coast, the other along the eastern slope of the Rocky Mountains. They followed both. With regard to the Athapascans,
however, there is no doubt that only a few of them pushed
southward along the Pacific, a much larger number drifting
through countless years over the High Plains thoroughfare.

When white men first sailed along the northwest coast of
the United States region, one Athapascan tribe lived in
Washington, seven in Oregon, and eleven in northern California. They must have been there a long time, for their
culture was typical of those areas.[1]

Numerous ancient archaeological sites discovered on the
High Plains may have been, and some scientists believe they
were, occupied by Athapascans. The evidence denoting
their presence in these places shows that they were then, in
every sense of the word, true Plains Indians, in their customs, their economy, their characters, indeed, in every phase
of life. Needless to say, this plains culture had not been
acquired and developed in a brief span of years. And, it may
be noted, for example, that projectile points almost identical to those recovered at the High Plains sites have also been
found only a few miles from the Arctic Ocean, on the
Seward Peninsula of Alaska, and in Saskatchewan.

Drastic climatic changes which affected the lives of both
men and animals occurred on the High Plains. Over the
larger part of these changes, following the end of the Ice
Age, there was a long pluvial period, during which rivers

were large and lakes and swamplands existed. About seven thousand years ago the High Plains began to be hotter and drier. It is believed that the dry period peaked between six and five thousand years ago, but it persisted in mild form for at least five more centuries. The aridity had much to do with the disappearance of the Pleistocene mammals, such as the mastodon, the great sloth, the camel, and the giant bison. Probably they had become extinct in the region by 5000 B.C. But there were others to supplant them. The climate became relatively more moist, and deer, buffalo, elk, antelope, and many types of smaller game increased enormously, thriving on the seas of grass.

Except for the small number that followed the Pacific Coast from Alaska, then, the Athapascans moved southward from the immense Mackenzie River Basin, their route transecting the high open plains of Alberta, Saskatchewan, Montana, Wyoming, Nebraska, Colorado, Kansas, New Mexico, and the panhandles of Oklahoma and Texas. Perhaps some of them remained for a generation or two in localities where adequate food, fuel, and skins could be obtained. But in the end all of them moved on, seeping southward like ink through a blotter, for no tribes speaking the Athapascan tongue settled permanently between northern Canada and Nebraska.

Some of them chose to establish a homeland along the rivers of far western Nebraska, as is evident from archaeological discoveries and incidents occurring in the late seventeenth century. In 1682, Indians on the Mississippi River told Robert Cavelier, Sieur de La Salle, of fierce tribes that lived far to the west. The famous French explorer recorded their names as *Gattackas* and *Padoucas*. Oto warriors from Missouri informed Father Louis Hennepin, who was with La Salle, that raiders dwelling near the western mountains had used long spears when attacking them. The priest thought at first that the Oto were speaking of Spaniards, but it would be understood in time that they were telling him of the Padouca Apache, who used lances in battle. Before the time of La Salle, of course, these Plains Apache had become mounted Indians, and their reputation as belligerents had spread among tribes as far distant from their homeland as Illinois. In invading the midwestern prairies they were not only plunderers but revengers acting in retaliation for raids conducted against them by the Kansa, Pawnee, Oto, Caddoans, and other peoples.

Toward the southern end of the Rocky Mountains, in eastern Colorado or northeastern New Mexico, an important branch of the Athapascans's migration trail turned toward the southwest. There is no certainty where it left the plains and entered the mountains. Some investigators think it passed through the San Luis Valley of Colorado, crossed the Continental Divide, and descended the San Juan River into New Mexico. Other scholars believe it left the plains in northeastern New Mexico, ran through passes in that area, crossed the Rio Grande in the vicinity of Taos, and went on west over the Jemez Range into the San Juan Basin. Whichever way it went, the Navajo traveled over it, separated forever from their blood relatives who also had come from the far north. The other fork of the trail continued on southward, splitting into numerous affluents, and over it went the Apache. Some did not stop until they had reached southern New Mexico, northern Mexico, extreme western Texas along the Rio Grande, and, eventually, Arizona.

But besides those who had stopped in Nebraska, others spread out in southeastern Colorado, western Kansas, Oklahoma, and northern Texas, and these were the branches of the great family that would be known as the Plains Apache, controlling territory more than eight hundred miles in length from north to south, and varying in its east to west width from two to four hundred miles.

3

Twenty-two identifiable Plains Apache groups are known to have controlled parts of Nebraska, Kansas, Colorado, Oklahoma, New Mexico, and Texas in the first century of Spanish explorations (1540–1640) of this great region. Not all of them merit the status *tribe*. Some were very small, comprising no more than two or three hundred persons dwelling in a restricted area, and these properly deserve the classification *band*. As will be seen, however, a few, notably the Lipan and Padouca, were large and powerful, and they ranged far, indeed sometimes hundreds of miles, on hunts, raids, or trading missions.

Almost all names by which Plains Apache groups and bands are designated were initially given them by Spaniards and are either corruptions of Athapascan words, Spanish idiom, or reflective of some Apache characteristic or custom. The Spanish were woefully inept when it came to recording with accuracy Indian names they heard, but being consumed by dreams of finding treasure, they probably did not care and made little effort to interpret or spell them correctly. In old Spanish documents several spellings appear for the same Apache group.

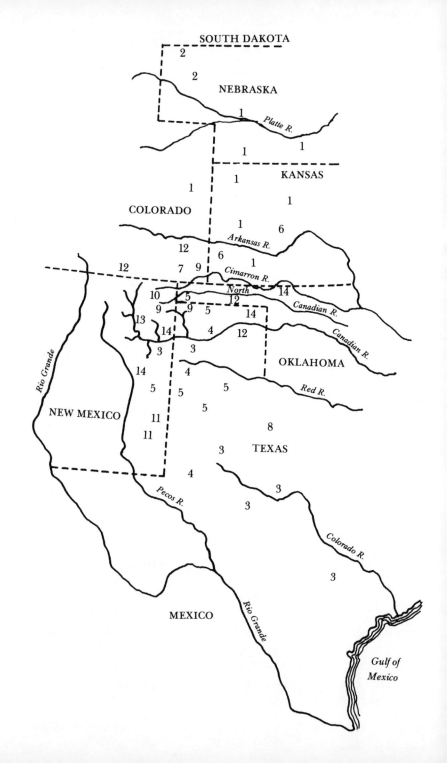

Plains Apache:
General Locations of Groups About 1700

1. Padoucas
2. Gattackas
3. Lipan
4. Teyas
5. Natagee, Lipiyane, Chipayne,
   Limita, Tremintina
6. Paloma
7. El Cuartelejo, Chalchufine,
   Carlana, Fleches de Palos, Penxaye
8. Cantsi
9. Conejeros
10. Achos
11. Perillo
12. Jicarilla
13. Rio Colorados
14. Faraons

Scale: 1 inch is approximately 150 miles

For many years the names Querecho, Vaquero, and Llanero—the latter signifying "people of the plains"—were
applied by various Spanish writers to the Plains Apache
groups of New Mexico and Texas. The French, but not the
Spanish, used the name *Padouca* to identify the Plains
Apache of Kansas and Nebraska. In numerous instances,
names appear once and vanish, being supplanted by others
totally dissimilar to them.

PADOUCAS: A powerful amalgamation of Plains
Apache bands in Nebraska and Kansas. The word at one
time was thought by some scholars to have derived from
Panateka, the name of a Comanche subdivision, but subse-
quent research has shown this to be in error. The Padoucas
occupied their Nebraska-Kansas homeland for centuries
before any Comanche invaded it. The meaning of the name
is not known. They were enterprising traders and notorious
raiders, venturing northward to the Missouri River in South
Dakota, eastward into the realms of the Caddoan Pawnee
and the Siouan Kansa, Osage, and Oto, and southward into
Oklahoma and Texas.

GATTACKA: They were the strange Athapascan band
that would become better known as the Kiowa-Apache. The
first written mention of them is in La Salle's accounts of his
explorations of 1682, when he heard of them from Indians
he encountered on the Mississippi near the mouth of the
Missouri. The identity of his informants is uncertain, but
they spoke of the western Indians they were describing as
Gattacka. The significance of the term is unknown. Later
French *voyageurs* would learn that it was the name by
which the Pawnee identified the Kiowa-Apache.

The Gattacka and the Kiowa in La Salle's time are
believed to have been occupying territory north of the
Nebraska Padoucas, in the vicinity of the Black Hills. For
many years before their name came to the notice of French

traders, they had been going periodically from that region to trade Spanish goods and horses with tribes, notably the Arikara and Mandan, on the upper Missouri. Obviously, therefore, they were in contact with other Plains Apache groups living close to New Mexico.

Some early accounts confuse the Gattacka with the northern Padouca, but the Gattacka belonged to another branch of the Athapascan family. They called themselves *Naichan*, and in identifying themselves the Lipan used the name *Naizhan*. The almost complete similarity of these names indicates that the Gattacka, or Kiowa-Apache, were indeed originally Lipans. But there is even better evidence to support this belief: The Gattacka themselves insisted to French traders that they were Lipans.[1]

LIPAN: One ʼof the largest divisions of the Plains Apache, they wandered over the Llano Estacado of eastern New Mexico and Texas, southeastward in the Colorado River Valley (Texas), perhaps to the vicinity of San Antonio and Corpus Christi, and, reportedly in prehistoric times to the lower Rio Grande, where they traded with coastal tribes. Some Spanish documents of the sixteenth century state that they traded with tribes *toward Florida*, which at that time included the Gulf of Mexico coast of Texas. The name *Lipan* derives from *Ipa-n-de*, the first part of the word believed to be a personal name, and the second part meaning "people." Caddoan tribes called them *Cantsi*, a name also adopted by the French. They were the first Plains Apache to be called *Querechos* by the Spanish, that name being recorded in the accounts of the Coronado Expedition.

TEYAS: A powerful Plains Apache group of western Texas and eastern New Mexico living in close association with the Lipans, and probably a branch of them. In the early sixteenth century they waged such a fierce offensive against pueblos south of Santa Fe that many of them were abandoned. One contributor to the Coronado papers states that the Teyas were at war with the Querechos, which indicates that he believed them to be another people, therefore, not Plains Apache. However, the so-called war may have been nothing more than a family row; certainly the Plains Apache fought among themselves. Some ethnologists have contended that the Teyas discovered by the Spanish in the Texas panhandle were originally Caddoans, an agricultural people who lived in northeast Texas in permanent towns, and that they had migrated west and joined the Lipans. If that is true, the Teyas Coronado encountered had completely forgotten the Caddoan culture, for they were full-fledged plains Indians, nomads subsisting entirely on buffalo, other game, and wild vegetal foods, and whose customs, habits, and traits were identical with those of the Querechos. In recent years linguists and other scientists have offered studies that identify the Teyas as Plains Apache, and bolstering their contention is the fact that Pueblo Indians, whose ancestors suffered so greatly from Teya raids, used the name *Teyas* in speaking of the Lipans. Perhaps the question of the Teyas' identity will never be resolved to the satisfaction of all scholars, but none of them can dispute that from *Teyas* came the word *Texas*. Whatever may be the truth, the Teyas of the far western Texas plains vanished in the early historical period, before linguistic evidence incontrovertibly proving their identity could be recorded.

NATAGEE, LIPIYANE, CHIPAYNE, LIMITA, TREMINTINA: These Plains Apache bands wandered over eastern New Mexico and adjoining parts of western Texas, largely south of the Texas Panhandle. *Tremintina* means "turpentine," but how the name could be applied to a primitive people is a mystery. The significance of the other names is unknown. While each of these bands had its own leaders and was autonomous, as late as the eighteenth century, if not later, they maintained close political and military relationships.

PALOMA: As the name not only means "dove" but "pleasant" or "mild person," one well may wonder how it came to be applied to a Plains Apache band. The Paloma dwelt mainly in extreme western Kansas, although they have been mentioned as living also in southeastern Colorado. Their Apache name is unknown.

EL CUARTELEJO, CHALCHUFINE, CARLANA, FLECHES DE PALOS, PENXAYE: When first encountered by Spaniards, these bands lived in southeastern Colorado. *El Cuartelejo,* presumably signifying "faraway quarter," was a name the Spanish gave to an area of southeastern Colorado and western Kansas, but it also was applied to a prominent band of Plains Apache living there. *Carlana* was the name given by the Spanish to the influential leader of a band. The significance of the other names is unknown. Perhaps *Fleches de Palos* indicated some type of arrows. These bands, all of which are believed to have been relatively small, were generally friendly to the Spanish, in hope of obtaining their assistance in combating raiders.

CANTSI: This band dwelt in western Texas. The name, sometimes called *Cances,* was applied to them by the Caddoan tribes of northeastern Texas, and was used at times to indicate the Lipan. Although the Cantsi were a group in their own right, they most probably were a branch of the Lipan.

RIO COLORADOS: The Canadian River, along which this band lived in northeastern New Mexico, was called *Rio Colorados* by some early Spanish explorers.

CONEJEROS: A band that roamed over northeastern

New Mexico, western Kansas, and southeastern Colorado. Except that they lived in close proximity to numerous other groups, nothing is known of them. Their name may have developed from some Spanish word or term indicating a type of dwelling.

ACHOS: As far as known, this band, probably very small, lived in northeastern New Mexico.

PERILLO: Southeastern New Mexico was the home of this band when first encountered by the Spanish. They must have lost their individual identity at an early date, for nothing more is known of them.

JICARILLA: They called themselves *Tindé*, "the people." They are known to have ranged in late prehistoric times over a large area, from the Arkansas River in Colorado into Oklahoma and northern Texas, and westward into the high mountains of northeastern New Mexico. They may very well have been the last major group of Athapascans to migrate to the southwest from northern Canada. *Jicarilla* was a Spanish word indicating "little basket," and it was applied to this band because of the expertness with which their women wove these receptacles. They were close blood relatives of the Lipan.

FARAON: Variations of this name (Pharaones and Pharoahs) first appeared in Spanish dispatches between 1672 and 1675. At the time this band ranged along the Rio Pecos, perhaps from the pueblo called Pecos in northern New Mexico to extreme southeastern New Mexico. It is known that between 1690 and 1725 they still maintained rancherias on Ute Creek, but after that period their locations are obscure. It seems certain, however, that eventually they were absorbed by the Mescalero. Modern linguists place them with the Mescalero group of the Western Apache. Early Spanish explorers undoubtedly encountered them in eastern New Mexico but did not give them a separate designation, perhaps including them under the general term *Vaquero*, for they were then typical buffalo-hunting Plains Apache.

4

It was a strange but enduring alliance, that of the Kiowa and the tribe that would become known in history as the Kiowa-Apache. Strange because the Kiowa sprang from two distinct linguistic stocks, the Tanoan and the Shoshonean, and the Kiowa-Apache were Athapascans. But not only their respective languages were alien; they were also peoples of contrasting cultures, with differing beliefs and traditions. Yet for at least three centuries, and perhaps for a longer time, they were inseparable.

In prehistoric times, long before they knew white men lived on earth, the Kiowa made their homeland at the head of the Missouri River, near the present Virginia City, in southwestern Montana. That was as far back as their tradition went when French *voyageurs* eventually met them in the far northern plains and mountains. By this time, in the seventeenth century, the Kiowa-Apache had long been incorporated into the social, economic, and political structures of the Kiowa.

The Kiowa-Apache migrated southward from northern Canada, through the Mackenzie River Basin, electing to

follow a route that took them southeastward through
Alberta, east of the Continental Divide, into Montana, and
on to the realm of the Kiowa, along the Madison and Jeffer-
son and Gallatin Rivers. Perhaps they were forced westward
from the Montana plains into the mountains. Their Athapascan predecessors, the Lipan and Jicarilla, to whom they
were closely related, had been able to follow a trail along
the High Plains east of the Rocky Mountains. It seems prob-
able that the Kiowa-Apache, lacking strength in numbers,
found themselves too weak to attempt a passage through
northern High Plains territories controlled by much larger
tribes, and abandoned all hope of reaching their own people
farther to the south. Moreover, it was unlikely that they had
any knowledge as to where the Jicarilla and the Lipan had
established themselves, how far to the south they had gone.

In any case, the Kiowa-Apache found a haven among the
Kiowa, and they would never leave them.

Traditions that must be heeded with extreme caution,
and a few old but seemingly creditable records, profusely
illustrate the story of the Kiowa and the Kiowa-Apache after
their amalgamation. The Kiowa always claimed that after
they and their Athapascan partners emerged from the northern mountains they formed an alliance with the Crow. That
cannot be correct. The Crow had not reached their homeland on the Yellowstone River in southern Montana before
the last quarter of the eighteenth century, and possibly not
until the early years of the nineteenth century. The first historical mention of the Kiowa-Apache was made by La Salle
in 1682, a hundred years before the Crow had migrated
westward from the Missouri. And at that time, according to
the information La Salle obtained, the Gattacka, or Kiowa-
Apache, were in the region that would become a part of
western South Dakota with the Kiowa, whom the French
explorer called *Manrhoats*.

There seems to be little doubt that the Gattacka were

closely related to the Sarsi of Saskatchewan. The Kiowa-Apache told early traders that they were gradually pushed southward by the Arapaho and Cheyenne. The Dakota Sioux claimed that they had driven the Kiowa and Kiowa-Apache southward from the Black Hills.

Now some well-established facts begin to emerge. In 1840 the Kiowa and Kiowa-Apache made peace with the Arapaho and Cheyenne, and troubles between them ended forever. When the Kiowa and Kiowa-Apache reached the Arkansas River, presumably in western Kansas, they found their way blocked by the Comanche, who claimed all territory to the south. Strained relations endured for a time, but the Comanche, realizing the value of having the notorious Kiowa raiders as allies, subscribed to an amnesty. Thereafter, the Kiowa and the Kiowa-Apache rode with the Comanche on plundering forays through western Oklahoma, western Texas, and eastern New Mexico. By this time most of the Plains Apache who had for so long controlled this vast region had been destroyed or driven out of it. Not infrequently the combined Comanche–Kiowa–Kiowa-Apache raiders struck deep into Mexico, at times as far south as Durango.

Between 1868 and 1875 the survivors of this once powerful and deadly triumvirate were driven onto an Oklahoma reservation.

The story of the Kiowa-Apache remains incomparably unique in Indian history, for after uniting with the Kiowa they were never again associated in any way with other Athapascans. Yet, even at the time of their ultimate capitulation to the Americans they were still speaking their own tongue, and still paying obeisance to their own ancient gods.

PART TWO

The Indé

1

Only on the shores of the seas did wind blow as constantly as on the High Plains. In summer the wind came at times like withering blasts from the door of a flaming furnace, usually moving southwesterly or southerly, perhaps blowing in bands of no more than a few yards to a half mile in width, with belts of less terrific heat between them. In the autumn not infrequently they came from the southeast. In the winter and early spring they might sweep down from the north, carrying with them a solid sheet of black clouds, blinding swirls of sand and dust, sleet and snow, unimpeded in the monotony of the land-seas reaching away to an ever-distant horizon, tearing and gnawing at every living thing, man, animal, and plant, that cowered feebly before them. And then suddenly, in both summer and winter, they would stop—but not for very long—as if withdrawing in a respite among the mountain walls and peaks that created another kind of climatic world in the west.

For thousands of years the annual precipitation of the High Plains has been low (and still is), often no more than ten inches, and seldom as much as twenty inches. But the grasses that grew there, the grasses now called *bunch*, and grama, and buffalo, usually received enough moisture to survive in their respective natural states. They were admirably suited to withstand conditions of excess moisture, excess drought, and fires that would have destroyed other species of plants, especially trees. Trees could live only adjacent to streams where there was seepage water, and only in the protection of barrancas into which moisture trickled and was held. And as there were few streams and deep ravines, so there were few trees.

Vegetarians could live on the High Plains only because the grass was dependable. Carnivores could live there because they could sustain themselves on the prey they desired. The Plains Apache could live there because in the scheme of this natural life they found a place for themselves, they found the ways and means of utilizing the bounties of the land as did the beasts they devoured. Both the animals and the people suffered scarcities, both enjoyed times of plenty, each depending one upon another in the pattern of existence, and each in its own peculiar way defying the meteorological forces that constantly menaced them.

The Plains Apache made good use of all animals, large and small.

The burrowing rodent, whose relative, the marmot, whistled danger in the mountains, squeaked alarms at the entrances of village channels that wove superbly engineered, complicated passages beneath dry surfaces. They were a main entrée of the carnivora, a supplement in the diet of the people, but their flesh added a definite taste to a heterogeneous dish. They needed little water and lived on grass, pulling it out by the roots. Americans would give them a name totally alien to their true genus. To settlers from the east they appeared to be big, plump underground squirrels, but the only squirrels with which these emigrants were familiar climbed trees, and this was a zoological contrast that left them totally baffled. *Prairie squirrels* would have been a fitting name for them, but in their dilemma the Americans called them *prairie dogs*.

The speed of the antelope and the keenness of its sight were greater by far than these attributes in any other animal. It was the truest creature of the plains, having developed there, and being unrelated to the antelope family of Europe and Asia. It flashed danger by contracting muscles on its rump and creating a white patch that could be seen for a great distance. Its meat being relatively delicate and savory, and its hide when properly tanned being soft and pliable, it was prized as a food and in the manufacturing of light garments, containers for personal possessions, and small utilitarian cases. But it was not easy to bring them down with arrows, and seldom could a hunter get close enough to spear them. Possessing great vitality even when struck, it might spring into flight and escape, vanishing into some distant tilt or ripple of the plains. Its greatest weakness was curiosity, an irresistible urge to investigate a strange object, and by capitalizing on this defect in its character a primitive hunter might be able to attract it within reach of his weapons, but only occasionally with success. It would become popularly known among white plainsmen as the *pronghorn*, and their rifles would be disastrous to it.

The High Plains swarmed with hares. Their powerful rear legs, much longer than their forelegs, not only made them exceedingly swift but also provided them with the ability to travel, if they wished, with long, graceful leaps. Customarily they ran in straight lines or in wide curves only for short distances, but often they attempted to avoid detection merely by crouching, making them comparatively easy prey. Their long, erect ears made white men think of burros, and they called them *jackass rabbits*, which became shortened to the popular name that would endure. They were not rabbits, but true hares, and it is believed they originated in the Great Plains environment. The Plains Apache ate them, but not with great relish. The soft fur, however, was utilized in numerous ways, especially in cradles and as decorative trimming on ceremonial costumes.

Wolves and coyotes, the cowardly enemies of all men and animals, were scorned as food by the Plains Apache, but the long-haired winter skins of the great gray wolf were used to some extent as cold-weather garments and as tipi bedding.

The deer was the second most valuable animal. It was not especially difficult to kill, its meat was delicious, and excellent and durable clothing as well as a great variety of household and travel articles, dog harnesses, pack straps, and trappings could be made from the skins. Venison also was an ingredient of foods prepared for preservation and storage.

The most valuable of all animals of the High Plains was larger than any other, a slow runner, clumsy, stupid, possessed of poor eyesight and only a moderately keen sense of smell. It was the bison, which Spaniards would speak of simply as the wild cows or cattle, and which later white invaders of the Great Plains would call *buffalo*, a name that as yet remains untraceable to a definitive origin. It was an ox, and, like *Homo sapiens*, it reached North America from Siberia over the Bering land bridge and migrated southward far back in the Pleistocene.

As it is said of the domesticated hog, virtually every part of the buffalo was used in some way by the Plains Apache, except the snort, and even that sound was imitated in hunting ceremonials. The meat, rich in fat and protein and unsurpassed in flavor, was baked, boiled, roasted, or eaten raw. Tongues, eyes, brains, tripe, hearts, and other internal organs were consumed. Blood went into puddings, stews, soups, and other dishes. Fetal calves, when very small, were a delicacy. Marrow, extracted by cracking large roasted bones, was savored. Lungs were boiled with vegetables, and grilled udders, with and without milk in them, were a special treat.

Always with a thought of trading with the Pueblos and other tribes to the west in the deserts where there were no buffalo, the Plains Apache preserved buffalo meat (as well as venison in smaller quantities) in two ways. Slicing it thin, they dried it on racks, and this would be the food that American westerners would call *jerky*. A combination of dehydrated buffalo meat and fat would be given the name of *pemmican* by early explorers and fur traders.

The merits of the two methods of preserving buffalo meat are explained by Tom McHugh in his authoritative work *The Time of the Buffalo*. Terming pemmican "the product of one of the most effective methods of food processing ever devised," he states that although jerky weighed only about one-sixth as much as fresh meat, "it was bulky—rather like a bundle of tree bark. In rain or damp air, it absorbed moisture readily, gaining weight as well as molding or decaying, often both. And if completely dry, it was hard to eat, calling for strong teeth and endless munching."

These drawbacks were eliminated in pemmican. McHugh continues: "After pulverizing jerky, the Indians packed it into bags sewed from buffalo rawhide, each one about the size of a pillow case. Into these sacks they poured hot liquid marrow fat, which seeped through the contents to form a film around each crumb of meat. The bags were stitched up at the mouth and sealed with tallow along the seams. Before the contents had time to harden, each bag was tramped or pressed into a flat shape about six or seven inches thick. A single sack, weighing about ninety pounds, was known as a 'piece' of pemmican, and made a convenient parcel for back-packing or portaging. It was also easy to store. . . . Plain pemmican, if properly made with only dried lean meat and rendered fat, lasted almost indefinitely."

Buffalo flesh was the chief food staple of the Plains Apache, and the buffalo was the chief source of articles they used and wore in their daily lives and paraphernalia of many kinds—even hooves were used as small utensils. Buffalo also were used for beautiful, warm, soft robes, other clothing, leather for countless articles, moccasins, shields, magnificently tanned skins for tipis, hair woven into blankets, scarves, bags, wallets, ropes, halters, lariats, belts, cords, medicine pouches . . . the list is endless. To it, however, should be added such important things as bags, trunks, boxes, dog saddles, straps, parfleches, ornaments, horn and bone ladles, and rattles made from buffalo scrota.

Being nomadic hunters, the Plains Apache did not practice agriculture to a great extent, although some groups planted small fields of beans, squashes, and maize in the spring, left to wander on the plains, and returned to harvest the crops in the late summer or the autumn. These vegetables were mixed with meat, as were the wild fruits, seeds, berries, tubers, and roots they gathered.

They hunted only to fulfill their needs, never killing animals for sport. Fish, bear, and beaver were not consumed, a custom the genesis of which is not known but which undoubtedly was due to cosmogonic and religious views that had long been forgotten before the advent of white men. In any case, there were not very many fish, bears, or beaver in the territory of the Plains Apache.

Their menu would undergo drastic changes as Spanish settlement pushed northward from Mexico. They would acquire a taste for domesticated animals, the single exception being pork, which for some unknown reason they distinctly disliked. Mule they craved, and roasted horsemeat ranked above mutton and beef. Not many years had passed after Spanish colonization began before the Plains Apache were sustaining themselves to a large extent on stolen livestock. Raiding Spanish herds and fields was easier than hunting wild animals.

2

One of several names by which the Comanche would call the Plains Apache was *Tá-ashi*. It meant "turned up," and it had reference to the toes of their moccasins. The moccasins were really a kind of boot, reaching nearly to the knees. Made of dressed buckskin, the legs had several folds which could be brought up to protect the thighs, and when not being worn in that manner the folds could be used to hold small implements and trinkets. The soles were thick, undressed hide with the hairy side out.

In hot weather, besides moccasins, the women wore light, loose buckskin clothing, but when it was cold they garbed themselves in fringed skin cloaks with the sleeves gathered up at the shoulders, wearing them over small petticoats. Their hair was allowed to grow long, hanging down the back in a plait, but for some religious ceremonials and dances it was unbound, flowing loosely over the shoulders. Shell and bone earrings and necklaces were worn, and clothing was decorated with dyed patches of animal skin.

The main garment of the men was a long breechcloth,

passing between the legs and hanging over the belt in both the front and the back. In winter they added a heavy shirt made of two skins, strapped in at the waist and hanging like a kilt, front and back. Facial hairs and eyebrows were plucked out. Both men and women painted their faces and exposed parts of their bodies in stripes, other designs, and daubs, using various colors.

A child was born with the mother in a kneeling position, midwives holding her firmly by the shoulders. The umbilical cord was tied close to the child's body, and the placenta was deeply buried at some distance from the tipi in which the birth took place. It was believed that lightning and a small whirlwind were the mysterious forces that gave breath and warmth to a new body, and that they entered it through the mouth as it emerged from the womb. After being anointed with a scented oily substance, a newborn child was held up to the four directions and displayed to the sun.

Among the Plains Apache, states W. W. Newcomb,[1] "Marriage was a contract between two families, with each member of the partnership having duties and responsibilities not only to the mate but to the mate's family. When a young man desired to marry a girl he was expected to obtain permission from her father, or brother, or some other male relative. But even though marriage was an understanding between families rather than between individuals, there was considerable courting of girls, and courting techniques included the use of a flute whose dulcet tones presumably softened the resistance of a maiden's heart. If the girl's parents agreed to the union, the bridegroom made them a gift. . . ."[2]

The marriage ceremony was private. A basin was constructed out of a large buffalo hide, which was taken to a secluded place and filled with water. Holding hands, the bride and groom stood in the water for a time. The parents of both of them appeared, considering them man and wife, and all returned to the bride's village, where a public dance was held.

Polygamy was practiced, but was largely restricted to chieftains, celebrated warriors, and affluent men. Thus, monogamy was predominant. According to Newcomb, "When a man's wife died he was not released from his obligations, and he remained under the control of her family. Normally they would provide another wife for him, either a sister of his deceased wife, or a cousin. The widespread custom of marrying a deceased wife's sister (sororate) . . . meant that a family's economic well-being was not jeopardized by the departure of a provider. Nor was a widow released immediately from her obligations to her deceased husband's family . . . and his family frequently produced a cousin or brother of her dead husband for her to marry." In polygamous cases, a man usually was married to several sisters, rather than having wives from different families.

Everything the Plains Apache made was designed and developed to meet practical needs and was adaptable to a nomadic life. They obtained pottery from the Pueblos, although some of the Plains Apache women made a crude type, but, except for small pieces, it was left in campsites to which they periodically returned, for it was heavy, easily broken, and difficult to transport. They were skillful and artistic basket makers, producing them in a large variety of shapes and sizes. Few Indians excelled the Plains Apache in manufacturing arrows and arrowheads and lances. Their weapons were things of beauty and demonstrated their superior craftsmanship.

They were excellent tanners. Tannic acid was a chemical unknown to them, but they achieved the desired results with other agents, concocted from such natural ingredients as cooked mixtures of grease and liver, greases of several types, pounded soapy roots, animal broth, and urine. The lightness, softness, and durability of the skins of their tipis and wickiups astounded the Spaniards.

The Plains Apache were not a people of large stature. Most men were of medium height; those standing two or three inches over six feet were exceptions. They were spare, lithe, and possessed of extraordinary stamina and remarkable muscular strength. Most females were several inches shorter than the average male. Many young women were noticeably attractive, displaying grace and having slender figures, but unending hard work, childbearing, and a precarious existence usually took a heavy toll of their bodies by the third decade of life.

Drawing on numerous sources as well as personal experience, Charles F. Lummis would write,[3] "Not of imposing height, most warriors were straight, compact, strongly built, but seldom heavy; and always of that easy carriage that belongs alone to perfect physical condition. Their arms and legs were smooth and round; rarely scrawny and rarely fat. A grand depth and breadth of chest and generous substantiality of back were observable in all.

"The head was fairly well molded and of good size. The straight black hair was generally trimmed at the level of the shoulder blades. The features were strongly and rather sharply marked; the aquiline nose not generally heavy, nor the lips over-full. The eyes were sparkling, restless, and unfathomable. The face was never blank, yet never legible. It seemed as if the nerves and muscles by which, in civilization the brain reflects its images upon the countenance, had all been cut. There was not a twitch, a shade, a change by which the keenest could read what was behind.

"Meantime, through this impassive mask he was searching your very soul with indifferent eyes that never looked at you. He kept the senses which nature gave man, and he educated them as few of us are ever educated in anything. No sound was so faint, no trace so delicate, as to escape his notice; nor, noticed, to elude his comprehension. A pebble with its earthward side turned up, a broken plant, the invisible flash of a gun miles away—he noted and understood them all. He would stoop to a trail so dim that the best Caucasian observer would not dream of its presence, and tell correctly how long ago that imprint was made. The arid hillside or the dust maze of the trail were an open book to him, with full detail of when and how many passed, Indians or whites, men or women, night or day. He was always learning from nature at first hand. He earned the eye of the kite, the ear of the cat, the cunning of the fox, the tirelessness of the gray wolf."

On the High Plains, burning sunlight, dry air, almost ceaseless activity, and a nourishing diet of proteins, fats, vegetables, and fruits contributed to the normal good health of the Plains Apache. Viral and communicable diseases, such as smallpox, measles, scarlet fever, diphtheria, tuberculosis, and syphilis were unknown among them until after the invasion of their homeland by white men and Indians who had been exposed to these virulent afflictions. However, they were not immune to arthritis, neuralgia, pleurisy, pneumonia, and various functional disorders. Ophthalmic conditions due to smoke and sand and osteomyelitis and periostitis due to bone injury and infections from wounds were suffered by them. Because they moved frequently, sanitation was not a problem. Indeed, wherever they stopped, either for long or short periods, it was their custom to perform their bodily functions at a distance from their tipis ;.ud campgrounds.

Until the coming of their destroyers, most of the time the Plains Apache lived well, prospering from their trade and their labors. Adverse weather conditions, which caused wild foods to fail and scarcities of animals, brought inescapable hardships, but these were temporary situations, and the

Plains Apache invariably found means of enduring them.
Not only their spiritual but also their social activities were
rich, rewarding, and pleasant. They held numerous ceremonies, engaged in many communal dances, and were addicted
to sports and games of chance, such as races of all types,
wrestling, and throwing dice. They were inveterate gam-
blers.

They attached great importance to what might be termed
the family circle, displaying profound affection for their
children. Yet, being realists, they were unsparing in training
their sons and daughters to counter and overcome the vicis-
situdes they understood would surely confront them. The
young Plains Apache was taught to show no more compassion or consideration for a human adversary than for a bug
or animal, to conceal all sensitivity to suffering, to subjugate
emotion to cold-blooded reaction. The law of the natural
world was kill or be killed. The supreme law to which man
must adhere was to retaliate in kind. Any deviation from
this code was an invitation to disaster.

The Plains Apache were one people, but they were not
politically united nor universally governed. There were no
permanent supreme tribal leaders, although there were
chieftains of both large and small groups. Chieftainships
were hereditary, usually gained through clan and blood
lineage, but some men achieved high positions as rewards
for their wisdom and leadership ability. Bands that were
united in wartime or for the purpose of conducting raids
were controlled by appointed commanders, but when the
purpose for which they had amalgamated no longer existed,
dissolution occurred. Descent was in the female line, and
each person belonged to the clan of his or her mother. Ex-
ogamy was strictly maintained, and marriages between persons of so-called related clans were prohibited, even though
the relationship was not consanguineous. Some clans took
their names from birds or plants, but the names of most
were descriptive of geographical features.

The religion of the Plains Apache speaks of a class of supernatural beings believed at one remote time to have lived as people on the earth. Because of sickness and death, these deities set out in search of a place without disease. They found it, and with it eternal life. But its location is uncertain, and the supernatural beings may have separated, some finding the perfect world they sought in certain mountains, and others in underground realms, each domain belonging exclusively to those who had discovered it.[4]

The Plains Apache recognized a supreme being with the power of creation, but as he was neither benevolent nor punitive he was not worshiped. They had no conception of a hereafter, such as the Christian heaven and hell. Their religion was a system of imitative and sympathetic magic aimed ritually at fulfillment of the requirements of life and living. When death came, man and woman became one with the cosmos, a condition in which they were neither punished nor rewarded; it was the normal end of the life cycle for them as it was for plants and animals—water poured into a stream was no longer identifiable.

Every Plains Apache religious ceremonial was designed to accomplish a specific purpose. Some were prophylactic in nature and conducted to ward off evil or attract goodness. The Plains Apache endeavored especially to appease the Evil Spirit. The picture of a god that was all good was incomprehensible to them.

Prehistoric trade trails were long, in the west reaching from the Pacific Coast to the Mississippi, from the Gulf of Mexio and the Sea of Cortez (Gulf of California) to the northern Great Plains. The Plains Apache, ranking among the most enterprising traders of all Indian peoples, maintained a flow of robes and hides, jerky, pemmican, tallow, and leather goods to other tribes in the mountains and deserts and plains adjoining their High Plains homeland. Pecos and Taos pueblos were visited seasonally by them, and they were active in this commerce through the length and breadth of the great Rio Grande watershed. In exchange for their goods they received turquoise and other semiprecious stones, ornaments made of a variety of materials, maize, calabashes, beans, cotton cloth, paint pigments, all manner of utensils, and coral and shells.

The great distances some of these products traveled is indicated by the fact that when the Spaniards first encountered the Plains Apache in New Mexico, northern Texas, Colorado, Kansas, and Nebraska, they found abalone shells from the Pacific among them, and when the French first reached the northern Great Plains, Indians there possessed the same species of shell.

3

These people are called Querechos and Teyas. They travel around near the cows, killing them for food. They live in tents made of the tanned skins of the cows. They did nothing unusual when they saw our army, except to come out of their tents to look at us . . . and asked who we were. The country is like a bowl, so that when a man sits down, the horizon surrounds him all around at the distance of a musket shot. The number of cows is incredible.

Pedro de Castañeda, the author of the lines above, was a private soldier for three years (1540–1543) in the expedition commanded by Francisco Vásquez de Coronado. Very little information about his personal life has come to light. He was a native of Logroño Province, Spain. Circumstances suggest that he was a young man, perhaps no more than sixteen, when he sailed for Mexico. The extent of his education is unknown, but, obviously, he attended school somewhere long enough to learn to read and write. He was one of the colonists who settled at San Miguel, Culiacán, which was founded on the west coast of Mexico in 1531, but the type of work he did has not been ascertained. Apparently

Coronado's Expedition, 1540–1542

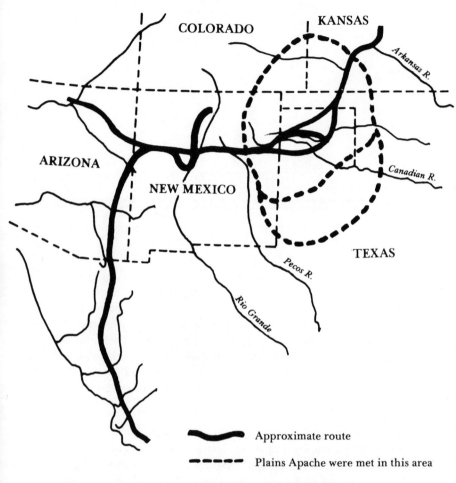

COLORADO   KANSAS

Arkansas R.

ARIZONA

NEW MEXICO

Canadian R.

TEXAS

Pecos R.

Rio Grande

⬛〰️⬛ Approximate route

▬ ▬ ▬ Plains Apache were met in this area

Scale: 1 inch = 215 miles

Culiacán was his home when, in 1540, he volunteered to
serve under Coronado in the search for the treasures
believed to exist in the unknown land north of Mexico.
Only a hint as to the time of his death has come down
through the centuries. In 1554, his wife, four daughters, and
four sons petitioned the government of New Spain for com-
pensation in payment for the services he rendered the King
on the northern exploration. It is not a matter of record
whether their claim was honored or rejected, but it seems
reasonable to assume that they would not have filed the
legal action in their own behalf had he still been living.

Castañeda's narrative of the Coronado Expedition is of
transcending importance, for it provides detailed descriptions of southwestern Indians as they were in the fourth
decade of the sixteenth century. Of inestimable value, in the
case of this work, is his account of the Plains Apache.[1]

Cicuyé was the great pueblo that would become better
known in history as Pecos. It stood on the Pecos River, near
the present New Mexico community of the same name.
Coronado and his gold-mad adventurers, leaving a trail of
disaster and death behind them among the Pueblo Indians,
had reached it early in the summer of 1541. The notorious
conquistador's goal was *Quivira*, a country far distant across
the Great Plains. There, according to Indians who hoped to
destroy him, incalculable fortunes in precious metals were
to be found.

For more than a year the progress of the expedition had
been marked by extreme hardships and fierce fighting. Some
of Coronado's officers and many of his soldiers had voiced
strong doubts that anything of value would be discovered.
Casualties had been heavy. Spaniards had been slain by
Pueblos struggling desperately to save their homes, families,
and meager possessions, and others had died of exposure,
malnutrition, infected wounds, and various illnesses. There
had been talk of abandoning the conquest, but Coronado

had held stubbornly to the conviction that somewhere in the vast unknown land ahead riches awaited him. He had shut his ears to the talk of turning back.

A few days after traveling eastward from the high mountains about *Cicuyé*, the High Plains, stretching into oblivion, had come into view. This was the beginning of the country of the Plains Apache, and the expedition encountered them first near the eastern boundary of New Mexico.

That the Querechos and Teyas "were very intelligent," wrote Castañeda, "is evident from the fact that although they conversed by means of signs they made themselves understood so well that there was no need of an interpreter."[2]

Castañeda recorded that the Querechos "said that there was a very large river over toward where the sun comes from, and that one could go along this river through an inhabited region for ninety days without a break from settlement to settlement. They said the river was more than a league wide and that there were many canoes on it."[3] Here was evidence that the Querechos were familiar with Indian canoes, a means of travel which they did not possess and could not have used on the small, swift streams of the High Plains. From their description of it, the river of which they were speaking must have been either the lower Arkansas, the Missouri, or the Mississippi, all hundreds of miles away.[4]

Castañeda thought the Plains Apache had better figures than the Pueblos, and Coronado concurred, in a letter to Viceroy Antonio de Mendoza expressing the opinion that their physiques were the best of any he had seen. They clothed themselves with buffalo skins, and from them they made ropes and obtained wool for weaving. From buffalo sinews they made thread with which they sewed their clothing and their tents. From buffalo bones they shaped awls and other tools. Dried buffalo dung was used for fuel. Buffalo bladders served as jugs. They ate the meat of animals both roasted and raw by taking a piece in their teeth and pulling it taut with one hand, in the other hand holding a flint knife with which to cut off a mouthful.

Castañeda wrote: "They travel like the Arabs, with their tents and troops of dogs loaded with poles and having Moorish pack-saddles with girths.[5] When the load gets disarranged, the dogs howl, calling someone to fix them right.

"These people dry the [buffalo and deer] flesh in the sun, cutting it thin like a leaf, and when dry they grind it like meal to keep it and make a sort of sea soup of it to eat. A handful thrown into a pot swells up so as to increase very much. They season it with fat, which they always try to secure when they kill a cow. They empty a large gut and fill it with blood, and carry this around the neck to drink when they are thirsty. When they open the belly of a cow, they squeeze out the chewed grass and drink the juice that remains behind, because they say that this contains the essence of the stomach. They cut the hide open at the back and pull it off at the joints, using a flint as large as a finger tied in a little stick, with as much ease as if working with a good iron tool. They give it an edge with their own teeth. The quickness with which they do this is something worth seeing and noting.

"There are very great numbers of wolves on these plains, which go around with the cows. They have white skins.[6] The deer are pied with white. Their skin is loose, so that when they are killed it can be pulled off with the hand while warm, coming off like pigskin. The rabbits, which are very numerous, are so foolish that those on horseback killed them with their lances.

"A Teya was seen to shoot a bull right through both shoulders with an arrow, which would be a good shot with a musket."

Castañeda considered the Plains Apache women "well

made and modest. They cover their whole body. They wear
shoes and buskins made of tanned skin. The women wear
cloaks over their small under petticoats, with sleeves gathered up at the shoulders, all of skin, and some wore something like little *sanbenitos*[7] with a fringe, which reached
half-way down the thigh."

The unbroken sweep of the Llano Estacado awed and
bewildered the Spaniards, and Castañeda would write that
whenever one looked at buffalo ahead "one could see the
sky between their legs, so that at a distance they looked like
trimmed pine tree trunks with the foliage joining at the
top. When a bull stood alone he resembled four such pines.
And however close to them one might be, when looking
across their backs one could not see the ground on the other
side."

There were some ravines, but they were never visible
until suddenly one came to the edge of a precipice and
looked down into them. In the ravines, some of which were
very deep and more like canyons, there were small streams,
and the trees were thick, and there were mulberries and
rosebushes and wild grapes and a type of wild fruit that
made the Spaniards think of Castilian prunes. Coronado
and his soldiers made wine from the wild grapes, and they
enjoyed drinking it while nibbling on nuts that resembled
walnuts, and they ate wild fowls, perhaps prairie chickens
and grouse and wild turkeys, all these things welcome relief
from the monotonous diet of buffalo meat and pemmican
and jerky, Castañeda's "sea soup."

Among the Teyas near Palo Duro Canyon, Castañeda
recalled, they saw "an Indian girl who was as white as a Castilian lady, except that she had her chin painted like a
Moorish woman. In general they paint themselves this way,
and they decorate their eyes."[8]

"It was impossible to find tracks in this country," said
Castañeda, "because the grass straightened up again as soon

as it was trodden down." Spaniards who went hunting were lost, and were found only with the assistance of Teyas, but some of the hunters "did not get back to the army for two or three days, wandering about as if they were crazy, in one direction or another." Every evening an account was taken "of who was missing, guns were fired and trumpets sounded and drums beaten and fires built." It is worth noting that the country is so level that at midday, after one has wandered about in one direction and another in pursuit of game, the only thing to do is to stay near the game quietly until sunset, so as to see where it goes down. . . .

"A tempest came up one afternoon with a very high wind and hail, and in a very short space of time a great quantity of hailstones, as big as bowls, or bigger, fell as thick as raindrops, so that in places they covered the ground two or three spans or more deep . . . there was not a horse that did not break away. . . ." Fortunately the expedition was in a deep ravine at the time of the storm, but if it had "struck them while they were upon the plain, the army would have been in great danger of being left without its horses. The hail broke many tents, and battered many helmets, and wounded many of the horses, and broke all the crockery of the army, and the gourds, which was no small loss, because they do not have crockery in this region."

From the vicinity of Palo Duro Canyon, with only a small company—perhaps thirty horsemen—Coronado had set out in pursuit of his dream, pushing steadily toward the northeast, across the plains of the Oklahoma Panhandle and southern Kansas. The main army was sent back to the Rio Grande to await his return among the Pueblos.

After traveling for some thirty days, existing entirely on game roasted over sputtering fires made of dried buffalo dung, the determined conquistador and his little band reached the Arkansas River at the point where one day the town of Ford, Kansas, would stand.

They found nothing, as Castañeda would recount, but "cows, grass, and sky." Still Coronado refused to abandon all hope. Crossing the Great Bend of the Arkansas at the ford which had been used for countless centuries by Indians and buffalo, they went on toward the northeast as far as the Smoky Hill River near the present town of Lindsborg, Kansas. There Coronado gave up.

As the Spaniards returning from Quivira passed through their country, the Plains Apache avoided them. The aspens on the high New Mexico mountains were beginning to turn gold when they rejoined the main expedition on the Rio Grande. For Coronado and all his once-powerful army—now tattered, weary, and completely dispirited—the great dream had been shattered. They could do nothing but wait through another bitter winter until the spring of 1542, when they would start on the long and sad march back to Mexico.

Four decades would pass before the Querechos and the Teyas would see another white man.

PART THREE

The Enduring Myth

1

The Iron Age civilization of Europe, feeling out and grasping with tenuous tentacles, had reached the land of the Plains Apache, leaving ineradicable marks to denote its advance, and forcing indestructible transitions upon their Stone Age society. It had come gently at first, indicated by nothing more than four weary, lost, friendly men passing across the southern fringe of the incredibly vast region, who asked for nothing but guidance, who vanished into the west as peacefully as they had come out of the east. Years numbering only one more than the fingers of a hand passed, and then, suddenly, the sounds had returned, the tempo accelerated, emanating noisily from the drums of insatiable desire, consuming greed, and willful cruelty, signaling a fierce and uncontrollable conflict between two cultures, two sets of mores, and two kinds of spiritual beliefs that were irreconcilable.

Still, for some time the Plains Apache had not suffered grievous injuries, for before they had heard the roar of the Coronado tempest they had known that the Pueblos had made a tragic mistake in attempting to stand against its fury, and when it reached them they had stayed out of its way as much as possible. Communications traveled with astonishing speed in the wilderness, and soon after the Pueblos had been mercilessly slaughtered and burned alive the Plains Apache knew of the atrocities. Before they had seen them with their own eyes they had known of such wondrous things as horses and the armor that no arrow could penetrate. Before they had heard the thunder and had seen the flashing fire and had smelled the acrid fumes they had been aware of the deadliness of the mysterious guns.

If they could not understand it, the Plains Apache were able to comprehend the dire potentialities of the menace. They could realize its inherent power. Fleeing Pueblos had told them what had happened, making them see what could happen, leading them to the reasoning that similar resistance might be as disastrous for them. It was their conclusion that nothing at all was to be gained by fighting before they were hurt. Their own situation was not to be likened to that of the Pueblos. The Pueblos along the route Coronado took lived in permanent structures, some very large and very old. These were their only homes, and in them were all their possessions, their food stores, their sacred underground ceremonial chambers (kivas), the material symbols of their spiritual beliefs, and around these towns were the little fields, the maize and bean and melon and cotton patches, on which they depended for their existence. The Plains Apache, following their nomadic way of life, could easily replace their necessities, the skin tipis, the sod and brush shelters, the garments, the utensils, the tools, for all of those things were provided for them in a raw state by nature from the realm of grass and animals through which they were free to roam.

And when the soldiers had gone away, and the confusion and the clamor had subsided, the Plains Apache went on with the business of living as they had always lived, hunting and applying themselves to their crafts, plundering when an opportunity arose, driving off intruding bands of Pawnee and Kansa and Oto and Wichita and Tonkawan, even fighting among themselves at times, and maintaining their lucrative intertribal trade. They remembered with vividness the magic they had seen and the knowledge that had come to them from another distant world, but not only with pleasure or a sense of achievement, for each memory remained invested with anxiety. They could hope that the incomprehensible white men would never come again, but always, under the burden of an irresistible inner pressure, they kept an eye on the horizon.

If the Plains Apache had heard of New Spain, of Mexico —and probably they had—it is doubtful if in the third quarter of the sixteenth century they were aware that it had become a land of turmoil. The possibility may not be dismissed altogether, for there were trade trails and other means by which such news could have been disseminated, yet it would be illogical to assume that even if they had known of the exciting events taking place so far to the south they would have understood their significance.

The truth was that uprisings of Mexico Indians—especially in the Mixtón War—political dissensions, the discovery of rich mines, the opening of vast new grazing and farming areas, defiance of royal decrees, and other forms of lawlessness had created internal problems that required the full attention of the provincial government. Steadily the frontier was being pushed northward from central Mexico. Towns mushroomed wherever minerals and good cattle ranges were found. Although the Indians fought courageously to hold their homes and fields, tribe after tribe succumbed to the insuperable forces. Uncounted thousands of them, in violation of Spanish laws, were enslaved and made to labor for mineowners, cattlemen, ranchers, and other types of commercial enterprises. Always priests were in the vanguard of the pioneers. Missions and convents were established in the wilderness, and soldiers were sent to protect them.

Fabulous strikes of silver and other metals were made in the state of Nueva Vizcaya (now called Chihuahua), not far south of territory occupied by some Apache tribes. Santa Barbara, a shabby, dirty town on the Rio Florida, was the trading center of the region. To it and the adjacent country swarmed men of every stamp—miners, cattlemen, farmers, padres, slave traders, and outlaws. Although almost no factual information about the lands to the north was available, the myth that it was as rich, or richer, than Mexico endured. Men argued, Why wouldn't it be? Hadn't treasures of every type been found throughout the conquered provinces, in the West Indies, from Mexico to Peru? Adventurers and missionaries talked constantly of pushing farther north, the first group looking for precious metals and slaves, the latter for more souls to be saved. Perhaps some advised that Coronado had found nothing of intrinsic value, but there were points to be advanced against that fact, indisputable as it was. Coronado may have been careless, or incompetent, or simply stupid about such things. Actually, no one knew exactly where Coronado had gone or whether the investigations he had made were thorough.

If the dreamers knew any details of the disastrous Coronado Expedition—which is extremely doubtful—they ignored them. Moreover, no printed histories or official reports were obtainable; indeed, there were almost no printed books, except for a few religious tracts, to be found in all Mexico.[1]

The plans and hopes and ambitions of the dreamers gazing northward from Mexico were held within limits not as much by irresoluteness as by legal complications. New laws that became effective about 1573 prohibited explorations and the establishment of new settlements in unorganized colonial possessions without royal approval. The statutes contained strict requirements. Only persons of good character, known to be devout Catholics, and who could be relied upon to treat Indians with kindness and justice, would be permitted to lead expeditions of discovery. Thus, not a great many persons, and especially not adventurers on the frontier, could meet the qualifications of the new code. Even padres, under its provisions, must be accompanied by soldiers on any venture they desired to undertake—an expensive procedure, for the government was required to furnish all supplies and equipment for them, besides paying the wages of the military.

It is beyond question that exchanges of intelligence were made between the Indians Coronado encountered and the tribes of Nueva Vizcaya and other northern Mexican states, and that they knew more about each other than Spaniards on any level, of any calling, knew about them. These assertions are unequivocally substantiated by documents bearing various dates between the years 1580 and 1600, all of which pertain at least in part to the Plains Apache.

2

In June 1581, a small company of riders, comprised of three religious, nine soldiers, and nineteen Indian servants, was following a dusty trail down the valley of the Rio Conchos, which formed a twisting crack through the high, arid ranges of Nueva Vizcaya to empty its alkaline waters into the Rio Grande. Drifting along behind them, under the care of *vaqueros*, were a number of pack animals, a few extra horses, and a small herd of cattle.

Before the summer had passed they would open a new gateway to the north, on much of their journey traveling through country never before entered by white men.

The padres were Agustín Rodrigues, Francisco López, and Juan de Santa María. None would live to return to Santa Barbara, the starting place of the expedition.

In command of the soldiers was Captain Francisco Sánchez Chamuscado, a veteran frontier officer sixty years of age. He would die in horrible suffering on the trail.

For ten years, Fray Agustín had ministered to the Conchos Indians at a convent in Allende, and he had been eminently successful in winning converts among them. His neophytes had given him considerable information about people who dwelt far to the north and who knew nothing about the Christian God. For some time he had held the hope that he could go among the idolatrous northern tribes. At last, in 1580, he wrote the Viceroy proposing that he and two of his colleagues be permitted to undertake the mission. The plan was approved, and Captain Chamuscado was assigned to accompany the padres with a military escort.

Captain Chamuscado's aide and notary of the company was Hernán Gallegos, a young man who had served in several campaigns against Chichimeco Indians. Although reared in relatively humble circumstances, Gallegos had acquired an education, and he was eager to achieve a station higher than that of a soldier in frontier service. He held the conviction that the discovery and exploration of "new lands" was the best way to gain the political power and the monetary rewards he so ardently desired. When Captain Chamuscado approached him in regard to the northern venture, he readily agreed to go, seeing it as "an opportunity commensurate with my purpose and ambition."

The account of the Rodrigues-Chamuscado Expedition written by Gallegos is one of the treasures of sixteenth-century exploration in the regions inhabited by the Pueblos and the Plains Apache, not only because of the dramatic episodes it contains but also because it cast light—although faint at times, to be sure—where in the world's knowledge total darkness had prevailed.

Gallegos would avow in his report to Viceroy Lorenzo Suárez de Mendoza that he and the other members of the expedition had gone forth with the thought in mind "to discover New Mexico and other lands where God our Lord was pleased to direct them, in order that His holy faith might be taught and His gospel spread throughout the lands which they, as your loyal vassals, might thus discover in His holy service and in the interest of the Royal Crown."[1]

That was true of the three padres. As to Gallegos's private ambitions, something more should be said. He was looking for minerals, and he found some. For seven or eight years after returning from the exploration, he waged an unrelenting campaign in Spain for the governorship of New Mexico, petitioning the King and the Council of the Indies for the honor and reward of colonizing the province. He also asked for financial aid, claiming that he had spent all of his personal funds in his efforts to serve his country, with the result that he had fallen deeply into debt. Although he was recognized by high officials as a man of ability and a legitimate contender for the post, he was not successful in his quest.

The Rodrigues-Chamuscado company turned up the Rio Grande from the mouth of the Rio Conchos. One day, in an Indian town, Fray Agustín inquired of the inhabitants if they had ever seen a white man. The reply he received astonished everyone. He was told, wrote Gallegos, that "a long time ago," three white men and a black man had passed that way. After forty-five years the memory of Núñez Cabeza de Vaca and his companions was still preserved by these people, who were Jumano Apache.

But no Europeans had passed over the trail that ran along the Rio Grande above El Paso del Norte. Northward from that place they traveled for several weeks through totally unexplored country, until they crossed the east-west route Coronado had followed on his way to Quivira.[2]

In September, the company was in the Galisteo Valley, a few miles south of the future site of Santa Fe, when the decision was made to visit the buffalo plains, which Indians had informed them lay a few days' travel directly to the east.

"We asked," said Gallegos, "what people lived in that region. . . . They indicated to us that the inhabitants of the buffalo region . . . lived by hunting and ate nothing but buffalo meat during the winter; that during the rainy season they would go to the areas of the prickly pear and yucca;

that they had no houses, but only huts of buffalo hides; that they moved from place to place; that they were enemies of our informants, but nevertheless came to the pueblos of the latter in order to trade such articles as deerskins and buffalo hides for making footwear, and a large amount of meat, in exchange for corn and blankets; and that in this way, by communicating with one another, each nation had come to understand the other's language.

". . . we realized that there must be good grazing in a place where there were as many buffalo as the Indians reported. . . . Taking up some handfuls of soil, they said that the animals were just as numerous as the grains of sand in their hands, and that there were many rivers, water holes, and marshes where the buffalo ranged. We were much pleased by this news.

"They also said that the Indians who followed these herds were very brave, fine hunters with bow and arrow who would kill us. But God our Lord inspired us with such courage that we paid no attention to what was said. . . ."

Fray Juan de Santa María, however, decided that as far as he was concerned a sight-seeing trip to the buffalo plains was of no immediate importance, and he announced that he intended "to return to the land of the Christians in order to give an account and report of what had been discovered to his prelate and to his Excellency, the viceroy." Although the other friars and the soldiers pleaded with him to remain, he refused to change his mind and departed alone. He had traveled only two or three days when he was slain by Indians, but the others, on the way to the buffalo plains, would not learn of his death until several weeks later, when they again passed through the Galisteo Valley.

Having been unable to obtain Pueblo guides, the expedition wandered in a circuitous route through the mountainous area between the Galisteo Valley and the Pecos River, which they reached in the vicinity of Anton Chico. This was considerably south of the place where Coronado and his army had crossed the stream.

Here they entered the country of the Plains Apache.

Gallegos tells of their first encounter with them in this way:

"Continuing down this same river four leagues we went toward a column of smoke which we had noticed. We wanted to see whether there were people there of whom we could inquire about the buffalo. We came upon a rancheria on this river in which we found fifty huts and tents made of hides with strong white flaps after the fashion of field tents. Here we were met by more than four hundred warlike men armed with bows and arrows who asked us by means of signs what we wanted. We replied that we were coming to visit them and that they were our friends; but they were intent upon fighting us with their arrows. We decided to attack them if necessary but did not actually do so, waiting first to see if they would accept peace. Although on the point of clashing with them, should they provoke us, we restrained ourselves, though there was no fear in us.

"So we withdrew our force to see what the outcome would be. Then we made the sign of the cross with our hands in a token of friendship, and the Lord was pleased to fill them with fear while inspiring us with renewed courage. When they saw that we made the sign of the cross as an indication of peace, they, too, made the same sign . . . they welcomed us to their land. . . . Fray Agustín dismounted and took a cross from his neck for them to kiss, in order to let them know that we were children of the sun . . . they soon began to rejoice and make merry, and to give us of what they had."

Gallegos supplies no tribal name for these Indians. He notes that his expedition spent a day and night among them, and that their number increased from four hundred to two thousand. If that is correct, it seems obvious that these Plains Apache were far less menacing than he makes out. In a fight, the little company would not have survived very long before an onslaught by such a horde of warriors.

Although the Plains Apache were friendly, they were not cooperative. Gallegos writes: "We asked them where the buffalo were, and they told us that there were large numbers two days farther on, as thick as grass on the plains . . . but not one wished to come along with us." In contrast with Castañeda's statements, Gallegos described them as a "semi-naked people." But, like Castañeda, he was impressed by their means of travel, writing, "They have dogs which carry loads of two or three *arrobas*,[3] and they put leather pack-saddles on these animals, with poitrels and cruppers. They tie the dogs to one another as in a pack train, using maguey ropes for halters. The packs travel three or four leagues per day. These dogs are medium-sized shaggy animals."

Leaving the rancheria, the company was soon lost on the Llano Estacado, and "wandered on bewildered." Fortunately they were able to find their way back to the Rio Pecos, where the Plains Apache were still encamped. According to Gallegos, their efforts to obtain guides again failing, they boldly "seized an Indian, bound him, brought him to camp, and handed him over to our leader so that we could start at once and continue our journey to the cattle. Noting that the Indians had become angry, we decided to prepare ourselves fully for battle. . . ."

But the Plains Apache made no attempt to rescue the captive, and with him leading them the expedition traveled on for another three days, at the end of which time they came to "some small pools where the Indians were accustomed to drink. We opened these pools with hoes, since at first they did not contain enough water for even one of our animals. By God's will, as these pools were opened, so much water flowed from them that it was sufficient for ten thousand

horses." Presumably their guide, although not choosing to
serve them, showed them this trick of the plains and had no
intention of letting them suffer greatly from thirst, although
Gallegos claimed they "had gone without water for forty
hours, and if we had been without it one more day we
should have perished."

The next day, which Gallegos states was October 9
(1581), they saw buffalo for the first time, great herds of
them drifting over immense plains in which there were
pools of brackish water and a small stream.[4] He described
them as being "as large as the [domesticated] cattle of New
Spain, hump-backed and wooly, with short black horns and
big heads. The bulls have beards like he-goats. They are
fairly swift and run like pigs. They are so large that when
seen in the midst of a plain they resemble ships at sea or
carts on land . . . the bulls must weigh more than forty arrobas each when three years old. Their meat is delicious and
to our taste as palatable as our beef cattle. We killed forty
head with our harquebuses, to be used as food. It is easy to
kill these animals, for as soon as they are wounded they stop
moving, and, on stopping, they are slain."

The statement that here they "learned that this valley and
its waters extended to the river where the great bulk of the
buffalo ranged . . . according to the natives . . . in astonishing numbers" indicates that they met more Plains Apache.
The river mentioned could have been either the Cimarron
or the Arkansas. They were tempted to journey to it, but
decided to forgo further exploration toward the northeast
because of rapidly diminishing supplies of maize and other
dried vegetables they had obtained from the Pueblos. Buffalo meat was delicious, but they had no wish to exist
entirely on it, and they had no stomach for the greasy and,
to them, unsavory pemmican of the Plains Apache.

They freed their guide, giving him presents with which
he appeared to be delighted, and turned back. Late in Octo-

ber they were again in the Galisteo Valley, where they had a skirmish with some unfriendly Pueblos. Passing through the mountains that rose to the east of the Rio Grande, they reached the many pueblos that stood along that river.[5]

Fray Agustín and Fray Francisco López announced that they had selected the pueblo of Puaray on the Rio Grande[6] as the site of the mission they wished to establish, and would remain there. To no avail, Captain Chamuscado pleaded fervently with them to return to Mexico with him and submit a report and a plan for the mission to the Viceroy. On a wintry day in January 1582, the two friars stood in their tattered robes before the gate to the old pueblo, made the sign of the cross, and waved farewell to their companions. They, and several Mexico Indian converts who had willingly agreed to stay with them, would soon be slain, presumably in a plot conceived by jealous medicine men.

Captain Chamuscado, his hands and feet paralyzed, necessitating that he be borne on a litter slung between two horses, died when the company was only thirty leagues from Santa Barbara.

Gallegos and the other soldiers were greeted as conquering heroes, and some of them, overcome by the attention paid to them, let their imaginations run wild, recounting fabulous tales of their exploits, and hinting that they had discovered a land enormously rich in mines. Gallegos applied himself to preparing a report to be submitted to the Viceroy. Local authorities demanded that he submit his papers first to them, and when he refused they schemed to have him arrested. He and one of the company's soldiers, Pedro de Bustamante, narrowly escaped with the documents, reaching Mexico City in May 1582.

They were granted an audience by the Viceroy and presented him with numerous souvenirs, including "ores from the mines discovered" in the north, some of which "assayed at twenty marcos per hundred weight."[7] It was Gallegos's opinion that "we brought great relief and inspiration to the people of New Spain."

Gallegos's secrecy in Santa Barbara also brought great excitement to adventurers and officials on the northern frontier, and rumors rapidly spread that many gold and silver mines had been discovered by the Rodrigues-Chamuscado Expedition and that the expedition had taken possession in the name of the King of an immense untouched territory not only containing no end of minerals but also endless grass pastures, lush valleys, immense forests, countless millions of wild cattle, and great numbers of heathen Indians all eager to become Christians. Three padres and a handful of soldiers had succeeded where Coronado, with an army, had failed.

3

Three more companies of treasure hunters would undertake illegal investigations of parts of the High Plains between the years 1582 and 1594. They left for official records some new geographical, economic, and cultural knowledge, but nothing of any real importance. Their inclusion here, however, is merited because each of them made a unique contribution to the annals of the Plains Apache.

Antonio de Espejo was a blackmailer and a convicted murderer who had prospered as a cattleman, farmer, and horse trader in the Santa Barbara region. He had been sent to Mexico City from Spain in 1571 as a confidential agent of the Inquisition. Possessed of a complex character, he was brutal, highly intelligent and clever, and very persuasive. As a spy charged with exposing heretics and officials disloyal to the Church he had enjoyed an enviable income, but rumors persisted that a substantial part of it derived from unorthodox manipulations. Yet, when there appeared good reasons for suspecting him of accepting bribes, he was never called upon by Church authorities to defend himself against such an accusation.

He and his brother, Pedro, entering into partnership, had taken advantage of the opportunities proffered by the opening of the northern Mexico frontier, and had rapidly developed profitable enterprises. But even in that wild country their ruthless and violent actions had brought them serious trouble. They had shot to death two of their *vaqueros*. Both were charged with murder and taken to Mexico City for trial. Pedro had been sentenced to a term in prison, but Antonio—undoubtedly because the court had been aware that he was still active as a spy for the Inquisition—suffered only a fine. Instead of paying it, he fled back to Nueva Vizcaya, thus becoming a fugitive from justice.

Reports disseminated by members of the Rodrigues-Chamuscado Expedition had fired Antonio de Espejo's blood, and he had soon devised a scheme by which he believed he could acquire the mines allegedly existing in the country of the upper Rio Grande. It soon became apparent that because of his criminal record he could not obtain official authorization for the enterprise, but he had another card to play. Aware that the Franciscans were profoundly concerned about the two padres who had remained at Puaray, he offered to finance and lead a party to determine their fate.

Fray Bernardino Beltrán readily accepted the proposal and volunteered to obtain the necessary permit. There is no certainty as to how he accomplished the feat. One account states that it was issued by his superior, but another indicates that it was granted by the lieutenant-governor of Nueva Vizcaya. In either case, its issuance would not have been in compliance with the law. No less a personage than the Viceroy could legally authorize any type of exploration in the north.

Espejo prepared a small company that would be able to travel with speed.[1] The start was made on November 10, 1581, from Valle de Allende, a short distance from Santa Barbara. With Espejo and Fray Bernardino were fourteen soldiers—one of whom insisted on taking his wife and three small children with him—a number of Indian servants, a small packtrain, and a herd of one hundred horses. Although Espejo had agreed to pay all costs and wages and to supply all equipment, he decreased his own investment by selling some shares in the project to Nueva Vizcaya politicians.

Among the soldiers were two brothers, Gaspar and Pedro de Luxán, and the latter would keep a diary. It is the most reliable account of the expedition,[2] since the report Espejo wrote contained exaggerations and claims that liken it in some respects to a chamber of commerce document.

Pressing ahead rapidly down the Rio Conchos, by late December the company was following the trail along the Rio Grande in New Mexico. There they came upon Indians who told them that Fray Agustín and Fray Francisco López had been slain at Puaray.

Some of the members wanted to turn back, but Espejo refused, bluntly stating that rescuing the two friars had been only one purpose of the journey. He enumerated several reasons for continuing. Already they had heard from Indians that provinces in which mines abounded were ahead, both to the east and the west of the river. And he did not fail to remind his companions that they were blessed with an opportunity not only to become rich but to serve God, Church, and King in a way that would bring them great spiritual satisfaction and personal honor.

They went on. From the pueblos in the vicinity of the present Albuquerque they rode in the dead of winter westward, passing Acoma and Zuni, to the Hopi villages in northern Arizona. There Espejo was told that gold mines were to be found far to the southwest, beyond many difficult ridges, and over a route on which there was a scarcity of water. Espejo demonstrated his own daring and courage. On a day late in April 1583, with only four soldiers and several

Hopi guides, he set out to find the mineral deposits, sending the other members back to Zuni to await his return.

Espejo would discover the great mines along the Verde River in Arizona which in later years would yield immense fortunes, but he thought them of no value. Luxán, who had gone with him, would record that they were "so worthless that we did not find in them a trace of silver, as they were copper . . . and poor."

They returned by a more direct route to Zuni. There they found Fray Bernardino and several soldiers determined to leave at once for Mexico. A violent argument took place, and Espejo was the loser. The padre and six men departed.[3]

Espejo with eight soldiers, one of them the chronicler, Luxán, and a few servants who had remained loyal to him retraced their trail across New Mexico, on the way engaging in several fights with unfriendly Indians. Somewhere along this route he became determined to see the buffalo plains, and in July, after passing through the Galisteo Valley, he reached the Rio Pecos on the edge of the country of the Plains Apache.

At the river he apparently changed his mind, for instead of continuing on east he turned south. Now, as he had done when he went in search of the Arizona mines, he was traveling through a land never before seen by white men.

Through the intense summer heat they traveled for several hundred miles along the Pecos. It would be illogical to believe that they were not seen by the Plains Apache in all this distance, yet it would be their claim that they saw no other human beings until they were in the vicinity of Toyah Lake in western Texas. There, fortunately for them, they came upon three friendly Jumano Indians whom they were able to make understand that they wished to go to the junction of the Rio Grande and the Rio Conchos. The Jumanos showed them the way, and they arrived in the

Valle de Allende, their starting place, on September 10, 1582, having been gone approximately eleven months.

Luxán reported that all the land along the Rio Pecos was "very level, containing fine pastures and many water holes . . . we found many buffalo tracks as well as bones and skulls. . . . In all this trip we did not find any buffalo, nothing but many tracks . . . we were greatly troubled by lack of food." Espejo, however, would write that they had seen "great numbers of native cattle." In view of other claims he made, this statement must be looked upon with suspicion.

But there is one sentence in Espejo's account to the Viceroy that is of paramount importance. He was the first to point out that carts and wagons could be driven through the Plains Apache country.

4

In the late sixteenth century a series of menacing international incidents made it imperative that Spain pay serious attention to guarding the northern flank of its immense New World dominion. British raiders had struck along the Pacific Coast, threatening the lucrative commerce that had been established and was growing rapidly between Mexico and the Orient. Explorers from several European nations were probing the opposite side of the continent. There were rumors that the mythical Strait of Anian, believed to reach from the Atlantic to the Pacific across northern North America, had been discovered, and that England was planning to fortify it, and thus would control a new and shorter route from Europe to the Far East.

Several months before Espejo had returned to write of the wondrous resources he had found, King Philip had revealed that he wished to have practical measures taken toward the founding of a permanent colony, appropriately garrisoned, in the undeveloped region north of Mexico. In a royal cedula to the Viceroy he had stated the belief that the best procedure, and perhaps the most economical, would be to

contract with some responsible person to undertake the conquest, a man who was not only wealthy, devout, and of good
repute but who would obey the laws controlling colonization and who had fully demonstrated his ability to serve as
the first governor of the province of New Mexico.

Only a saint could have come close to meeting these specifications, and there were few, if any, blood-and-flesh saints
in Mexico. There were, however, any number of men who,
if their records for integrity and responsibility were somewhat stained, could qualify as being wealthy and prominent.
And anyone could swear to uphold the laws and attend
church on holy days. As the King's idea became known, proprietors of great estates, mineowners, magnates of commerce, political and military officials—indeed, the affluent
and the distinguished in every state of Mexico—became
embroiled in feverish competition for the coveted post.
Fearing royal displeasure, and far more cognizant than the
sovereign in far-off Seville of the tremendous organizational,
legal, and political complications involved in such an
immense project, the Viceroy and his confidants were careful to make no hasty decisions. In fact, more than a decade
would pass during which they gave themselves to thoughtful
deliberations and argued so much with each other that little
or nothing was accomplished. Meanwhile, the files of the
Council of the Indies bulged with communications regarding the northern conquest. The tension was increased,
moreover, by the appointment of a new viceroy, Luis de
Velasco. Despite the growing urgency, he refused, on the
grounds that he was unfamiliar with the problem, to make
blind decisions, or even to acquiesce to the opinions
expressed by his advisers. He announced that he would
make known his views in due time, but only after conducting his own investigation.

Undoubtedly a number of men, some of whom had lived
for six or seven years with the hope of being chosen, had

been tempted to take matters into their own hands, much as Espejo had done.[1] But the risks were great, costs would be extreme, and they had no assurance that success would relieve them from suffering penalties. Certainly they would not escape the wrath of others seeking the office, many of whom were politically powerful.

Gaspar Castano de Sosa would boldy defy these justifiable fears and move independently.

A pioneer in northern Mexico, he had founded several settlements, had been the first *alcalde* of Monterrey, and later lieutenant governor and captain general of the state of Nuevo Léon. As unscrupulous as he was aggressive, he had acquired, by both legal and illegal means, mining properties and ranches, and he had engaged in the Indian slave trade. Twice, at his own expense, he had sent emissaries to Mexico City in futile attempts to induce the provincial government to award him the authority to colonize New Mexico. The only response he received was a command from the Viceroy to stop capturing and selling Indian slaves and a warning not to leave Mexico without official permission. Although he realized no less than his competitors the perils inherent in an unauthorized conquest, he was blinded by visions of accumulating great riches, and he permitted his greed to overcome his good sense.

Castano was the owner of extensive cattle ranges and agricultural lands in the vicinity of Monclova, where he made his home. He invited townspeople and tenant farmers, all of whom were mired in a state of poverty, to a fiesta. After stuffing his ragged guests with good food and wine, he informed them that he had learned confidentially about bountiful lands to be taken for nothing, and he proposed that they join him in an expedition to occupy them. Everyone who went would become the owner of a large rancho. And there would be other rewards. So rich was this northern country in minerals that with little work they would all become inconceivably wealthy. To show that he was telling the truth, he displayed pieces of extremely high-grade silver which, he swore, had come from unowned mines on the upper Rio Grande.

The silver trick worked. Dancing for joy, the ignorant peons, who had no hope of possessing more than a mud hut, a straw bed, and a few animals, agreed to go with him to the land of promise.

Castano and his colonials would participate in the first recorded clash between white men and Plains Apache in which blood was shed and deaths occurred. The company would take the first wheeled vehicles, including two small brass cannon, into the Plains Apache country. The enterprise represented the first attempt to establish a permanent colony in the American Southwest, and for all involved it ended in tragedy.

A column composed of one hundred and seventy men, women, and children—virtually the entire population of Monclova and its environs—a train of supply wagons, and large herds of horses, cattle, goats, and sheep crawled in a cloud of choking dust and terrible heat toward the Rio Grande in the late summer of 1590. Riders were sent ahead to capture some Indians and enslave them. Now the hopeful peons had the first taste of the affluence they expected to enjoy—they had servants, all their own.

Completely a victim of his own illusions, Castano disdained to follow the long-established trail along the Rio Conchos. He harbored the idea that if he opened a new route he might come upon treasures previous explorers had missed. As a result, it took some six weeks for the company to find a passage to the Rio Grande. The river was reached at some point between the present Texas towns of Del Rio and Eagle Pass, and almost insurmountable difficulties were encountered in getting the heavily loaded carts and wagons across the soft, sandy sinks on each side of the stream. So exhausted by this ordeal were the colonists and animals that it was necessary to spend two or three weeks on the east bank to let them recover their health.

It was early October when they moved on. The country in places was impassable, and numerous detours had to be made. Stubbornly Castano insisted on pushing toward the northeast, for reasons known only to himself, refusing to follow the better trail that ran northward along the Rio Grande. At last, after several more weeks of struggle, they came to the Rio Pecos. Traveling northward along the river with greater ease, they entered the Llano Estacado, in the country of the Plains Apache. Now they were on the trail over which Espejo had returned.

The chief source of information about the Castano Expedition is a *Memoria,* the author of which has not been definitely identified.[2] According to this document, the company ran into serious trouble early in November with Plains Apache, at some point along the Rio Pecos. Descriptions of the country in the account are vague, but the conflict probably occurred near the present border of New Mexico. Apparently Castano had attempted to take shortcuts, moving away from the river to avoid its long bends—actually neither he nor anyone else with him knew whence the stream came or its course—causing all persons and animals to suffer severely at times for water.

The *Memoria* states that several men sent to search for missing horses discovered "some large salines with incredible amounts of very white salt. We spent the night along marshes formed by water from the river, which emptied into them in considerable volume."[3]

On the previous day they had come upon "a number of newly deserted rancherias. One lone Indian appeared and approached the wagons, but not a single interpreter of the many brought with us could understand him. . . . Castano ordered that he be given some corn and asked him to summon back the people of that vicinity, telling them not to be afraid. So he left. . . ."

But the lone Indian did not return, and it was not until they had camped near the marshes that they saw in the distance "some natives who were traveling." Some men were sent to overtake them, and they "brought back four persons; the rest fled and hid. . . . These natives had with them some dogs laden with packs, as is the custom in that region, a novelty none of us had ever seen before." After a futile attempt to obtain information about the country from them, the four captives were given some corn and meat and released.

On the following day, scouts "who were leading the way crossed the river [Rio Pecos] upon reaching an impassable spot, at which moment they saw a group of Indian men and went toward them. We all began to talk to the group by signs, some from one side of the river and some from the other. Our men drew away from the Indians, but Juan de Vega, himself a native [Mexican Indian], lagged behind. Some of the Indians, seeing he was alone, seized him, took some ropes away from him, threw him into the river, and shot him with three arrows. The next morning a large number of Indians appeared, and Castano tried in every way to get them to come to the camp, but to no avail.

"While we were in this place, the men in the camp noticed the Indians driving away some oxen. Castano ordered six [mounted] soldiers to go after the thieves. During the pursuit, the soldiers encountered a group of Indians who attacked them with arrows. Our men in self-defense killed some of the assailants, apprehended four, and brought them to camp. Castano ordered that one of the prisoners be hanged as punishment and that the other three, since they were mere youths, be kept as interpreters. Despite our extreme care they escaped . . . with an ox."

It was late December when Castano and an advance guard came in sight of the great pueblo of Pecos. They had encountered no more Plains Apache, but now new trouble arose. The company's supplies of grain exhausted, Castano asked the inhabitants for maize. His request refused, he attacked, but not until an assault lasting several days, in which many Pueblos were slain, were his men able to break into the pueblo and plunder its stores.

From Pecos, the expedition turned westward, traveling through deep snow and in bitter cold toward the Rio Grande. After visiting numerous settlements and examining the country, Castano selected the Keres pueblo of Santo Domingo[4] as the "capital" of the colony he planned to establish. The entire company was settled there before mid-March 1591. Castano and a group of men were away searching for gold mines when Indians they met informed them "that many other Spaniards had arrived, which pleased us all very much." But their pleasure was of short duration. They were on their way back to Santo Domingo when messengers met them with bad news. Captain Juan Morlete, with a force of fifty cavalrymen, was waiting at the pueblo to arrest them.

Morlete carried instructions from the Viceroy. They said in part, "You will put a stop to the expedition planned and undertaken by Gaspar Castano in contravention of my specific order as well as the general orders of his Majesty. . . .

"When by God's favor you reach Gaspar Castano and his people, you will use every mild and prudent means you can to persuade them to give up their expedition and return with you. . . . You will bring them back in reasonable comfort; but you must always remember that you are conducting them as prisoners whose lack of conscience and evil aims you cannot trust . . . you will impound all goods belonging to the prisoners . . . you will bring everything to this capital [Mexico City], including all their wagons. If there are women in the company of the accused, you will see to it that they are well treated, and that their personal decency is

respected. . . . This same kindliness and good treatment
shall be shown to any children . . . you will take away from
Castano and his people any slaves they have seized and will
return these slaves, as you proceed to the places whence they
were removed or wherever they wish to go."

Castano's colony had existed hardly more than a month.
On an April day, when the valley of the Rio Grande was
beautiful with the full flowering of spring, the weary and disappointed colonists, the trail-worn livestock, and the creak-
ing wagons, all guarded by Morlete's cavalry, started down,
the long trail to Mexico. Castano, his legs in irons, rode in a
cart. The colonists, penniless and helpless, would be freed,
but Castano would be sentenced by the Audencia [judicial
court] of Mexico to serve six years in exile in the Philip-
pines. He would be killed there in a revolt of galley slaves.

5

In February 1593, Captain Francisco Leyva de Bonilla was sent with a contingent of cavalry to hunt for Indians who had been raiding cattle herds on Nueva Vizcaya ranches. Unbeknown to his superiors he had been conspiring with a disreputable adventurer, Antonio Gutiérrez de Humana, to go to New Mexico illegally and explore for silver mines. Somewhere in the barren country along the Rio Conchos, Humana joined him with a group of men and Mexico Indian servants who had been secretly recruited for the venture. A few of Bonilla's cavalrymen refused to become deserters and turned back, but most of them were induced to go along by promises of rich rewards.

The company, well armed and supplied, proceeded at a rapid pace, following the trail down the Rio Conchos to its junction with the Rio Grande. Turning up that river, they reached northern New Mexico in April, and established headquarters at the Tewa pueblo of San Ildefonso.[1]

From Pueblos, who undoubtedly were eager to be rid of the Spaniards, Bonilla and Humana heard that great fortunes in gold and silver were to be found in a province called Quivira that lay far across the buffalo plains to the east. They swallowed the tale with no less gullibility than Coronado had shown and set out to acquire the treasures with hopes no less feverish than those which had fired the great *conquistador* fifty-two years earlier.[2]

In May they passed Pecos Pueblo and entered the country of the Plains Apache. Beyond the Canadian River, in eastern New Mexico, they vanished on the grass sea of the High Plains.

The end of the story of the Bonilla-Humana company would not come to light until more than a decade later, but to avoid a disruption in continuity it will be recounted here.

Don Juan de Oñate of Zacatecas, a man of enormous wealth, distinguished lineage, and the heart of a beast, became the first governor of the province of New Mexico. He reached his post, which for so long had been sought by others, in the summer of 1598, establishing temporary headquarters in the Tewa pueblo of Ohke (the name of which he changed to San Juan de los Caballeros) on the Rio Grande a short distance above the mouth of the Rio Chama.

Oñate had orders to arrest Bonilla and Humana, but efforts to locate them failed. Indeed, all that could be learned was that they had disappeared in the country of the Plains Apache, and for five years nothing had been heard of them.

In February 1599, a Mexico Indian appeared and told a story that prompted his listeners to take him quickly before the governor. He said his name was Jusepe, his home was Culhuacán, a town about fifty miles north of Mexico City, and about six years earlier he had been engaged by Humana to serve him as a personal servant on a treasure hunt to the north.[3]

After leaving Pecos Pueblo, declared Jusepe, the Bonilla-Humana company traveled generally toward the northeast for about thirty days, passing without trouble many rancherias of the Vaquero Apache. At the end of that time they "reached two large rivers, and beyond them many rancherias with a large number of inhabitants. Farther on, in a plain, they came to a very large settlement which must have extended for ten leagues, because they traveled through it for two days, and it must have been two leagues wide, more or less. One of the rivers they had crossed previously flowed through this settlement. The houses were built on frames of poles, covered with straw. . . . They were built close together, along narrow streets, like alleys. However, in some places between the houses there were fields of corn, calabashes, and beans. The natives were very numerous but received the Spaniards peacefully and furnished them abundant supplies of food. These Indians obtained their livelihood from the buffalo."

After leaving the heavily settled region, proceeding in a northerly direction, "they came upon such a multitude of buffalo that the plain . . . was so covered with them that they were startled and amazed at the sight."

They obviously had passed beyond the customary range of the Plains Apache, and the people they encountered could have been Wichita, Kansa, or Osage. Perhaps they reached the territory of the Pawnee. The two large rivers of which Jusepe spoke could have been the Arkansas and the Smoky Hill or the Kansas and the Republican. They undoubtedly traveled considerably farther north than Coronado, and it is not improbable that they were the first Spaniards to enter Nebraska.

Somewhere in the heart of the Great Plains, Bonilla and Humana had a falling out, the cause of which was not known to Jusepe. As he recounted the event, the two men engaged in a bitter quarrel, after which Humana remained alone in his tent an entire afternoon and morning, writing, and at the end of this time he sent a servant to summon Captain Bonilla, who came dressed in shirt and breeches. Before he reached the tent, Humana went out to meet him, drew a butcher knife from his pocket, unsheathed it, and stabbed Bonilla twice, from which he soon afterward died. He was buried at once.

Humana appeared to have become mentally unbalanced, and fearing for their own safety under the leadership of the crazed outlaw, Jusepe and four other Indian servants deserted with the intention of returning to Mexico. Only Jusepe survived, the others being slain by unidentified Indians.

After wandering alone for some time, Jusepe had been taken prisoner by Plains Apache. He was made to work hard, but was otherwise unharmed. After a year in captivity he had managed to escape and make his way to Pecos Pueblo. When, after the passage of another year or two, he heard that Spaniards had established a settlement on the Rio Grande, he had set out to find them.

Still the whereabouts of Humana and other members of the company remained unknown. A rumor reached Oñate that, fearing to return and face punishment, they had gone farther north and were living with Indians, but it could not be confirmed.

Several more years would pass before the mystery was finally solved. After murdering Bonilla, Humana had led his men toward the southwest. Eventually they had reached the area in southeastern Colorado to which the Spanish would give the name El Cuartelejo. This was the home of a number of Plains Apache bands.

There in a cottonwood grove bordering a stream, a party of Spanish missionaries and soldiers came upon a number of badly rusted guns and swords which were identified as having belonged to the Bonilla-Humana Expedition. No human skeletons were found, but that was not strange, for animals would have devoured bodies and scattered bones that were not consumed.

A priest named the El Cuartelejo stream *El Rio de Las Animas Perdidas en Purgatorio,* the River of Lost Souls in Purgatory.

PART FOUR

The Growing Menace

1

In the name of King Philip, Governor Juan de Oñate had taken possession "of all the kingdoms and provinces of New Mexico." All that could be said about the size of the colony was that it was an enormous realm of plains, mountains, and deserts, the boundaries of which, except for that on the south, were lost in an infinity of sky. The Sea of Cortez (Gulf of California) could be reached by traveling a great distance to the southwest, but in other directions, that is, to the northwest, to the north, the northeast, and the east, only God knew how far it extended.

One of Oñate's first acts was to divide the province into mission districts, giving assignments to priests in such vague terms as in the west "the pueblo of Jemez and all Indians of the neighboring sierras and settlements," and in the north "the pueblos of Taos and Picuris and all Indians toward the north and east." Thus, the Plains Apache came under the jurisdiction of Fray Francisco de Zamora, but neither he nor his successors would see very many of them in the years immediately ahead, and no missions ever would be established on the High Plains over which they roamed.

This situation, unique in the American southwest, would

not be reflective at all of a lack of zeal in any missionaries charged with ministering to the Plains Apache. In almost every part of this vast region—indeed, in all the American west—Christian ecclesiastics would appear in prominent capacities, generally responsible for political, military, and religious actions, if not the final results, in which they participated. Quite to the contrary, the apostles who, following the colonization of New Mexico, accompanied expeditions to the country of the Plains Apache were precluded from implanting the doctrines of their religion in them by circumstances they had no means of combating. These involved such problems as remoteness from established routes of travel and communication, and the lack of both adequate military protection and logistical support. Yet, even if these difficulties could have been resolved, an even greater vicissitude would have confronted them: the indestructible determination of these people to resist to the death permanent intrusions upon their domain by either other red men or white, for any purpose whatsoever.

The dream of saving the souls of the Plains Apache would long endure, but many years before the dreamers finally abandoned it they would be constrained to confess—at least to themselves—that it would not be fulfilled.

Oñate was no less hopeful than any of the explorers who had preceded him of finding treasure in New Mexico, and the failures, of which he was fully apprised, deterred him not at all in planning to search for it. Having founded the colony and set up its political and religious structures, he did not intend to allow himself to be distracted by routine problems. He had brought with him aides whom he believed capable of assuming these burdens. Of the greatest importance was the task of learning as rapidly as possible what riches existed in the kingdom in which he was the supreme authority.

Ohke, or San Juan, turned out to be too small to accommodate the soldiers, priests, and colonists with the comfort they all desired, and they moved in the late summer of 1598 to the larger pueblos of Yunque and Yuque which stood one on each side of the Rio Grande, adjacent to the river's conjunction with the Rio Chama. The new capital was given the name San Gabriel. And there, at Yunque, the first Christian church in the southwest was built.

Settled in new and more commodious quarters, Oñate announced his plans for exploring the country. His nephew, Vincente de Zaldivar, would lead a company on a reconnaissance mission to the northeast and report on the buffalo and the people who subsisted on them. He himself would take an expedition to the west and southwest with three purposes in mind: to look for metals, to obtain pledges of obedience from Indians not yet visited, and to open a trail to the Gulf of California near the mouth of the Colorado River, from which place it was hoped communications by sea could be established with Acapulco or some other port on the west coast of Mexico.[1]

In mid-September, traveling generally eastward at a leisurely pace, Zaldivar reached Gallinas Creek (near Las Vegas, New Mexico), where he and his companions greatly enjoyed catching and eating trout. An account, probably prepared by Zaldivar's secretary for his signature, states that one evening five hundred fish were taken on a single hook.[2]

While they were encamped on the Gallinas, four Plains Apache warriors "came to meet them. The Spaniards gave them food and gifts. One of them arose and shouted to many others who were hiding, and all came to where the Spaniards were. They are sturdy people and fine bowmen. . . . Zaldivar asked them for a guide to the cattle and they furnished one very willingly."

This gesture of friendship was soon marred, however, by a demonstration that left no doubt that the Plains Apache, or Vaqueros, as Zaldivar called them, looked upon the Span-

iards as unwelcome visitors. Going on, they soon encountered more Indians who greeted them with menacing signs.
Jusepe, the former member of the Bonilla-Humana company, served as Zaldivar's interpreter, and he reported that
the Vaqueros "were very disturbed at seeing us in their
land. In order that they should not be further excited if
many people went among them, Zaldivar with only one
companion visited their rancheria, telling Jusepe to go on
ahead, reassure the people, and tell them he only wanted to
visit them and establish friendship with them."

The diplomatic effort was not immediately successful, for
there suddenly appeared "a ridiculous figure in human
form, with ears almost half a yard long, a snout horrible in
the extreme, a tail that almost dragged, dressed in a very
tight fitting pellico [skin garment], which encircled the
body and was all stained with blood; with his bow in his
hand, and quiver of arrows at his shoulder."

After a brief struggle, soldiers, acting on Zaldivar's orders,
succeeded in capturing the grotesque figure. His mask and
costume were removed, and he became a "very frightened
and embarrassed" Vaquero who confessed that he had
hoped to "scare us so we would flee and leave our baggage."

Shortly after this episode, according to Forbes,[3] Zaldivar's
"party came upon an Indian who was totally white, with
blueish eyes and a graceful and respectable appearance.
Behind him came a fair-sized party of Indian warriors. The
white Indian advanced without a word, and in an extremely
dignified manner he scrutinized the fifty Spaniards. Zaldivar, wishing to instill fear and astonishment in the Apache,
had one of his men discharge a musket. This apparently
intimidated the Indians."

Serious trouble fortunately averted, the Zaldivar expedition, comprised of sixty men, all heavily armed and well
supplied, their horses as well as themselves protected by
armor, followed a trail down the Canadian River. Numer-

ous groups of Plains Apache were encountered, but no more menacing incidents took place, and they began to see small herds of buffalo. Their guides informed them that at a certain place farther down the river a much greater number of buffalo would be found, but when they arrived there, "the cattle had moved away because a large number of Vaquero Indians who were returning from trading with the Picuries [sic] and Taos, populous pueblos of New Mexico, had just passed that way. The Vaqueros sold meat, skins, fat, tallow, and salt in exchange for cotton blankets, pottery, maize, and some green turquoises. . . ." In the coming years, seeking to gain full control of the lucrative commerce between the Plains Apache and the Pueblos, Spanish governors and missionaries, competing with each other, would only succeed in destroying it.

Zaldivar's report tells how he "came upon a rancheria of fifty tents made of tanned skins which were very bright red and white in color. They were round like pavilions, with flaps and openings, and made as neatly as those from Italy. They are so large that in the most common ones there is ample room for four individual mattresses and beds. The tanning is so good that even the heaviest rain will not go through the skin, nor does it become hard. On the contrary, when it dries it becomes as soft and pliable as before. As this was so amazing, he made the experiment himself; so, cutting off a piece of leather from a tent, he let it soak, then dried it in the sun, and it remained as pliable as if it had not been wet. He bartered for a tent and brought it to camp. And even though it was so large, as has been stated, it did not weigh more than fifty pounds.

"To carry these tents, the poles with which they set them up, and a bag of meat and their pinole, or maize, the Indians used medium-sized, shaggy dogs, which they harness like mules. They have large droves of them, each carrying a load of at least one hundred pounds. It is both interesting and amusing to see them traveling along, one after the other, dragging the ends of their poles, almost all of them with sores under the harness."[4]

Zaldivar had been instructed by Oñate to inform the Plains Apache that the country they occupied now belonged to the King of Spain, and through Jusepe he delivered the pronouncement in various rancherias. Oñate, he declared, "had sent him to tell them that those who remained loyal to his majesty would be favored and those who did not would be punished." The report's assertion that "all were left at peace and very pleased" is of questionable validity, to say the least.

What certainly was the greatest comedy ever witnessed by the Plains Apache—or any Indians, for that matter—was staged in the vicinity of the present Tucumcari, New Mexico, on an October day in 1598. Zaldivar had conceived the idea of capturing a herd of buffalo, driving the animals back to San Gabriel, and domesticating them on the pastures along the Rio Grande. The Spaniards looked about until they found "a good location for a corral and the material with which to build it. Having located a site, they proceeded to build the corral of cottonwood logs, which took them three days. It was so large and had such long wings that they thought they could enclose ten thousand head, because during those days they had seen so many cattle and they roamed so close to the tents and the horses. In view of this fact and that when they run they look as if they were hobbled, taking small leaps, the men took their capture for granted.

"The corral being completed, they set out on the following day toward a plain where, on the preceding afternoon, they had seen about one hundred thousand head of cattle. As they rushed them, the buffalo began to move toward the corral, but in a little while they stampeded with great fury in the direction of the men and broke through them, even though they held close together; and they were unable to stop the cattle; because they are stubborn animals, brave beyond praise, and so cunning that if one runs after them, they run, and if one stops or moves slowly, they stop and roll, just like mules, and after this rest they renew their flight. For a few days the men tried in a thousand ways to drive them inside the corral or round them up, but all methods proved equally fruitless. This is no small wonder, because they are unusually wild and fierce; in fact, they killed three of our horses and wounded forty others badly. They have very sharp horns, about one span and a half long, bent upward toward each other. They attack from the side, lowering the head way down, so that whatever they attack they gash easily. Nevertheless, many of them were killed. . . ."

With a throng of Plains Apache thoroughly enjoying the ludicrous spectacle, the Spaniards, wearied and dumbfounded but still determined, resorted to another scheme. "In view of the fact," states the report, "that the fully grown animals could not be taken alive, they took to catching calves, but the calves became so enraged that of the many that were brought along, some tied by the tail and others carried on the horses, not one got to within a league from camp alive, for all died within little more than an hour."

The Spaniards gave up, "for it seems that unless they are caught soon after they are born and mothered by our [domesticated] cows or goats, they cannot be taken until the buffalo become tamer than they are at present."

Like his predecessors, Zaldivar was told by the Plains Apache of a great river far to the east "that ran in the direction of Florida," but he did not set out to find it. The November winds blowing down from the high peaks of the Sangre de Cristo Mountains, already capped with snow, were chilling as he and his men rode back toward the colonial capital on the Rio Grande. He had not passed through unexplored territory. Indeed, he had accomplished nothing at all, except to advise the Plains Apache that they were now subjects of the King of Spain, and he had brought back nothing of value but an amazingly soft red-and-white tent and some two thousand pounds of buffalo fat, which would strengthen Spanish soups during the coming bitterly cold winter.[5]

2

Unlike the gun, the horse presented no mystery. It ate grass, and it left droppings, and its meat was edible, and its hide could be tanned, and it propagated and took care of itself. Thunder and explosion and fire were not required to give it life, to make it function.

Three-quarters of a century passed after the Plains Apache had first seen horses before they began to acquire them in appreciable numbers. They got them first largely by happenstance, perhaps one or two now and then by an advantageous trade, by good luck in gambling, by theft, by coming upon crippled strays—which they usually ate—but only a few over a period of years after the colonization of New Mexico. It is doubtful if any horses at all would have been found alive in their possession between the time of Coronado and Oñate, but the seventeenth century was not very old before a good many warriors were mounted and they were raiding far and wide, stealing from the herds of settlements, missions, and *estancias*, as well as from other tribes, striking in their forays from the upper Rio Grande into northern Mexico. For horses had become incomparable assets; not only did they equate the mobility of the Plains Apache—hence their striking power—with that of white and Indian enemies, but they were by far the most valuable of all articles of trade. Horses were riches.

It was the gun, of course, that in the end made it possible for the Plains Apache—for all Indians—to make fullest use of the horse, but the Plains Apache owned immense numbers of horses before they owned firearms, at least firearms that could be discharged. A gun without powder and lead was not as good a weapon as a war club with a flint spike in it or a bow and arrow. Guns could be stolen or captured, but obtaining adequate materials to make them work was extremely difficult. Moreover, solving the mechanics of these marvels and developing skill in using them were not tasks easily accomplished. The horse made it possible for the Plains Apache to travel long distances in commerce and war with what to them was almost incredible speed. The horse allowed them to increase immeasurably the quantity of their personal possessions. A pack pony could pull a *travois* loaded with a large tipi, robes, and utensils, and at the same time carry a squaw and several papooses. On trading missions the incomparably strong beast of burden could travel from dawn until dusk with a heavy pack of hides and other commodities, and in the evening it would refresh itself by rolling and drinking and restore its strength by cropping the sparse bunch-grass. The ranges of the Plains Apache country—indeed, the greater part of the American west—were a natural home for the horse. If the nutritious wild fodder failed or was destroyed by fire in one area, it could usually be found growing healthily in other places not far distant. Instinctively, like the buffalo, the horse migrated, following the grass and the seasons. Carnivores took a relatively small toll, for the horse was intelligent and swift, both means of self-protection, and when cornered was a vicious fighter. When, at last, it became possible for the Plains Apache to make effective use of the gun, the changes that transpired were no less significant than those wrought by the horse. Together the horse and the gun transformed the handicapped Stone Age warriors of the High Plains into formidable and skillful adversaries—as the Spanish, to their sorrow, would know through three lifetimes of attempting to conquer them.

By 1630, if not a few years earlier, the Spanish had given up all hope of preventing the Plains Apache from acquiring horses. The situation was far beyond possible control. Large herds of unbranded horses were grazing on the vast ranges of northern Mexico—"so many," said one report, "that they go wild in the country which ones are called *cimarrones*, some that live all their lives without an owner." As the Spanish continued to push northward—settlers, treasure hunters, trading expeditions—the number of wild horses steadily increased. Each year they were abandoned or lost in stampedes caused by buffalo, cougars, wolves, and marauding Indians. There is evidence indicating that by 1650 Spanish traders out of Mexico had ridden northward along the eastern base of the Rocky Mountains as far as southern Montana, and that there among the Kiowa and Kiowa-Apache they saw horses. Perhaps not very many, to be sure, but only a few years later tribes of the northern Great Plains owned enough horses to be called mounted Indians.

The Plains Apache had not been slow to recognize their opportunity to become wealthy. They spared no effort to round up wild horses while stealing them wherever they could, and they soon had become masters of the supply. They maintained a barrier through which they funneled them to other tribes dwelling farther north in profitable trade.

And their long struggle to maintain a stringent monopoly of this commerce would be one of the main causes of their downfall as rulers of the High Plains.

But this disaster was still considerably more than a hundred years ahead when, in 1601, Oñate made his first journey through the country of the Plains Apache, and he made no mention of seeing horses among them.

3

An account of the expedition Oñate took to the buffalo
plains in 1601 maintains that he went in accordance with
King Philip's pronounced desire to have "the most Holy
name of God and His holy gospel" carried to the "barbarous
nations, now in the power of Satan, the enemy of mankind."

This was the customary way of prefacing any document
dealing with an *entrada* into territory inhabited by uncon-
quered Indians. Invariably the avowal was superseded by
another purpose: to discover mineral treasures. And this
case was no exception. Oñate burdened himself not at all
with the work of saving souls.

However, besides his predominant hope of finding gold,
he was impelled to undertake the journey by a persistent
question for which he desperately wanted an answer. It was,
How far north did the land go? He was inspired by the idea
that he might have the good fortune to open a route to the
sea on the North, an accomplishment that would be of sur-
passing value to Spain, and would bring him both great
honors and monetary rewards.

Under Oñate's command was a group that left San

Gabriel on June 23. This group included his nephew, Vincente de Zaldivar, acting as his chief aide; Jusepe, once
again serving as guide and interpreter; two padres, Fray
Francisco de Velasco and Fray Pedro de Vergara; and "more
than seventy picked and well-equipped men; more than
seven hundred horses and mules, six carts drawn by mules
and two by oxen bringing four pieces of artillery, and
sufficient [Indian] servants to transport the necessary baggage."

Early in July, after passing through the upper Galisteo
Basin, crossing the Rio Pecos and the Rio Gallinas, they
reached the Canadian River, and "here we were met by
some Indians of the nation called Apache, who welcomed us
with demonstrations of peace. The governor and the men
with him treated them generously, so that, although at first
only a few came to meet us, within a short time men,
women, and children flocked to our camp and confirmed
their peaceful disposition by raising their hands to the sun,
which is their sign of friendship. They brought us some
small fruit, black and yellow, which abounds everywhere
along that river. These were the size of small tomatoes and
gave every indication of being healthful, for although we
ate them without restraint no one suffered any ill effects."[1]

At some point along the Canadian River, probably near
the Texas-Oklahoma border, the expedition turned toward
the north. For more than a fortnight they had seen large
herds of "cibola cattle"[2] and had feasted on them, and they
also had enjoyed quail, turkeys, venison, and the wild fruits,
plums, grapes, and berries that grew in profusion about
springs and in the folds of the plains sweeping away on
every side. They also had seen an amazing creature, "re-
sembling a deer and as large as a large horse, which roams
in herds of two and three hundred. Their deformed shape
makes one wonder whether they are deer or some other
kind of animal." They were probably elk.

Thus far in the country of the Plains Apache—perhaps Lipan, Jicarilla, and Teyas—no unpleasant incidents had occurred, although the expedition had encountered numerous people "who are masters of the plains. They have no permanent settlements or homes, but follow the cattle as they roam about. We had no trouble with them, even though we crossed their land, nor was there an Indian who ventured to harm us in the least, a favor of God our Lord, wherefore we never tired of praising and thanking Him. In gratitude, most of the men tried to make peace in their souls, and on Porciúncula day, which falls on August 2, most of the men confessed and took communion with particular devotion."

This agreeable situation suddenly ended.

They crossed the Cimarron River and pushed on northward in Kansas. Not infrequently, "the army strayed somewhat, which is not surprising, because the land is so level that people traveling over it got lost the moment they separated a little from us. For this reason it became necessary to send out men from certain places to explore. . . . To further reassure ourselves Governor Oñate sent the maese de campo [Zaldivar] ahead with some men, and with our usual good fortune, he soon came back, as he had found many signs of people and the land rich in pastures, the lack of which had concerned us most, since we had not found any for some days." Going on they came to a small stream, where they spent the night, and "the land was better than any we had seen, and the buffalo were so numerous that it was impossible to count them."

Zaldivar apparently had become extremely apprehensive, for "with the care and forethought which he, as a good soldier, always put into matters of war [he] organized and prepared his men for any eventuality." And on the following morning he set out again to explore the country ahead. After he and several companions had ridden six or eight miles they "discovered a large rancheria of more than five thousand people." This estimate of the number of Indians in the village seems excessive, if not beyond the realm of possibility. However, Zaldivar must have been sufficiently alarmed to inform Oñate promptly of his discovery.

The name *Apache* is not used in the Oñate account in connection with these Indians. The Spaniards would call them *Escanjaques*, because this word, or one that sounded like it to Spanish ears, allegedly was shouted by them when they raised the palm of their hands toward the sun, purportedly a sign of peace. However, linguists have been unable to find the word or a source from which it might have derived in any Indian tongue.

Nevertheless, the tribal identity of the Escanjaques can be determined with a large degree of certainty by evidence which, if circumstantial, must be recognized as conclusive. The finding rests on descriptions of their culture, their way of life, their dwellings, and their habitat, the area in which they lived and hunted.

Oñate encountered them in western Kansas, and in the early seventeenth century this was territory occupied and controlled by the Padouca tribe of the Plains Apache family.

Accompanied by the friars, Jusepe, and thirty heavily armed men, Oñate advanced toward the Escanjaques camp, and his chronicler noted that the "natives stood in good order before their ranchos, raised the palms of their hands toward the sun. . . . When we assured them that we desired peace, they all approached us, women and children, large and small, and allowed us to see their huts, which were made of branches about ten feet high placed in a circle. Some of the huts were so large that they measured more than ninety feet in circumference. Most of them were covered with tanned skins, which made them look like tents.

"These people did not plant or harvest, depending entirely for their food on the cattle. They were governed by captains, but being free men obeyed them but little. They had large quantities of skins which they wrapped around the body for clothing, but, as it was the hot season, the men went about almost stark naked, and the women clad only from the waist down. Generally they used bows and arrows, with which they were very skillful."

Jusepe had difficulty translating into his own Mexican tongue some of the words used by Escanjaques speakers, but others addressed him in a language he recognized as identical with that he had heard during his captivity among Apache. This is a significant statement.

Some scholars have expressed the opinion that the Escanjaques were Kansa or Osage. They seem to have overlooked certain important considerations: (1) The Kansa and Osage were traditional enemies of both the Apache Padoucas and Gattackas; (2) the homelands of the Kansa and Osage were in eastern Kansas and Missouri; (3) neither the Kansa nor the Osage would have reason to travel several hundred miles to western Kansas to obtain buffalo products, for enormous herds of these animals, as well as all other types of game native to the plains and prairies, were to be found in their territories; (4) if the Escanjaques had been either Kansa or Osage, it is illogical to believe that Apache warriors, free to act as spokesmen, would have been among them.

Unless he was a linguist of exceptional talent, Jusepe had not been long enough among the Plains Apache to have become fluent in their language. Moreover, dialects, phrases, and pronunciations varied greatly, just as they did, and do, in the branches of any Indian people who are scattered over hundreds, or thousands, of miles. Athapascans of Alaska and Arizona would have difficulty understanding each other. Even in the southwest of today the Athapascan

Navajo say the Athapascan Apache speak bad Apache, and the Athapascan Apache make the same accusation against the Athapascan Navajo.

Baltasar Martinez, a soldier with Oñate, said of the Escanjaques: "They have the same characteristics as the Apache, but are larger and more robust than the Mexicans; and they are dirty, dark, and of ugly features. They carry bows and arrows and hardwood war clubs three spans long with a large piece of flint at the end and a strap at the handle so as not to lose the club in battle. They have large buffalo shields to cover and protect the entire body."

Jusepe apparently had no trouble making the Escanjaques understand that Oñate knew Bonilla had been slain and that he was looking for Humana. The information startled them, and their manners and evasive statements made it clear that they assumed Oñate was intent upon punishing the Indians who had killed the explorers. At last they stated that Humana and his men had been ambushed "not a great distance away," but vehemently asserted that they had had nothing whatsoever to do with the killings. The murderers, they declared, were people who lived in a great town some twenty or thirty miles to the east and with whom they had long been at war.

Oñate had reached the frontier that separated the countries of two implacable and powerful peoples, the Plains Apache and the Caddoan Wichita, an area which could not be entered by members of either tribe without extreme peril.

Evidently Oñate heard conflicting stories about the fate of the Humana party, for the soldier Martinez would relate that the Escanjaques said the Wichita—whom he called *Rayados*—"were many, and their settlement large, and it took three days to pass through it, that in a hut there they burned Humana and his men, and that Oñate should be warned lest these people also burn him and his soldiers. The

Escanjaques said they wanted to accompany Oñate and fight the people of the great settlement. Oñate asked them for a guide and they said they would go with him themselves."

Still another story came from Juan Rodriguez, a Portuguese serving under Oñate, who recounted that the Escanjaques said "the people of the large settlement who had killed Humana were still holding one of his men who was sick and walked with a cane."[3]

The lies of the Escanjaques are understandable. They were eager to get the Wichita in trouble. Oñate, of course, having no other information about the Humana tragedy—years would pass before the truth was known—had no course but to continue his own investigation. He rejected the offer of the Escanjaques to accompany him to the settlement of the Wichita and ordered them to remain in their own rancheria, but unknown to him, they disobeyed.

Traveling northeast for a day or two, with Escanjaques scouts watching him, Oñate's force reached a fine, big river, with "marvelous level banks, but was so wooded that the trees formed very dense and extensive forests." It was the Arkansas.

In another day's travel down the river, according to the Oñate report, they "began to see people who stood on a hill." They were the Wichita, and "they advanced and challenged us to battle, shouting and throwing dirt in the air, which is the universal sign of war in this land. About three or four hundred persons awaited us, but, after an exchange of signs, we reassured them of our friendly motives and a few of them approached us and put about our necks some small strings of beads that they were wearing, declared themselves our friends, and invited us to their houses. We could not accept this offer that day since it was late. . . . They brought some ears of corn, the first we had seen in this good land, and some round loaves of corn bread as big as shields and two or three inches thick."

Oñate responded to these friendly overtures by seizing eight Wichita, one of them a *cacique* named Catarax.[4] They appeared to be greatly surprised when they were questioned about Humana, swearing that they knew nothing of his fate and that no Spaniard, either crippled or healthy, lived with them.

Now the Escanjaques boldly appeared "and shouted more challenges against the other nation than a Roldán could do while awaiting his chance to fall on the enemy. That night we watched with all necessary caution."

Martinez wrote: "Early the next morning, between six and eight hundred Escanjaques appeared at the camp, ready to fight, looking fierce in their war paint. Oñate asked them to stay together, but to keep away from the camp. The army crossed the river and marched toward the settlement followed by the said seven or eight hundred Escanjaques.

"When we came within view of the [Wichita] settlement, it was found to be deserted, as the people had fled. As soon as the Escanjaques became aware of this they rushed to the settlement in different directions and began to sack it and to set fire to the houses."

Oñate sent soldiers to stop the destruction, and the Escanjaques were driven from the town, being allowed to carry away with them only a small amount of corn. Oñate commanded them to return to their own country, and they departed in anger.

Both Wichita and Escanjaques had informed Oñate that farther east along the river were a great many other settlements with large populations. By some means, which is not made clear in the records, it was learned that the Wichita had fled for the purpose of summoning allies to join them in an attack on the Spaniards.

The Oñate account went: "The assembled Indians would be so numerous that an entire day would not suffice for them to leave their houses, and since we were so few, they said they would dispose of us in short order and not allow anyone to escape.

"We were obliged to hold a consultation as to what should be done. In view of the fact that the horses and mules were exhausted from so much travel, that the main purpose of our trip had been accomplished, that his majesty would be better served by learning of the greatness of this land so that he might take the necessary steps for his royal service and for the welfare of these souls, and since it would be folly for the few of us to go ahead where more than three hundred were needed, we all decided to present a petition to Governor Oñate, explaining the just causes for not proceeding any farther.

"It was a hard decision for Oñate to accept and he expressed strong feelings for halting the expedition, but in view of the justice of what was asked he granted it. . . ."

Martinez added another reason which played a part in Oñate's decision to turn back. The weather on the High Plains was getting cold, blizzards might soon sweep down from the north, and it "would be unwise to spend the winter in such a remote place."

Oñate led his men homeward, following the trail taken on the outbound journey. As they drew near to the rancherias of the Escanjaques, a contingent of twelve men, commanded by Zaldivar, was sent ahead to reconnoiter. The Escanjaques had not been seen since they had been forced to stop their plundering of the Wichita settlement, but now they suddenly made their presence known. Two of Zaldivar's soldiers were wounded in an ambush, and he and the others narrowly escaped with their lives.

The Spaniards were all well into the country of the Padoucas when the fight occurred. The Escanjaques' anger can be attributed to Oñate's refusal to permit them to destroy the Wichita town and carry off the valuable corn in its storehouses. Oñate would maintain that in spite of their "treachery" he had no wish to harm them, and that he attempted to convince them with "gestures of peace" that he would leave without further violence. In view of the large number of Escanjaques gathering about the Spaniards, this would have been wise strategy. However, whatever effort he made to avoid further confrontation was not successful.

The Oñate account continues: "The Indians, being eager for war, began the attack with great fury. In the first formation there were more than fifteen hundred natives, who, arranging themselves in a semi-circle, fought with great courage and determination. When the governor saw that the arrows came down thick, and that the enemy did not answer the sign of peace, he ordered his men to defend themselves. Both sides were now engaged in the battle, but God our Lord granted us the victory. Without His aide [sic] it would have been practically impossible, in view of the way the natives kept increasing in number, though our brave soldiers showed their outstanding courage and spirit and soon stopped the enemy attack, killing and wounding many who had taken positions in an arroyo.

"The Indians became more determined than ever and carried on for more than two hours with great bravery, although much to their cost, as they experienced the fury of Spanish power. In the end, most of our people were wounded, but no one critically. Seeing the savagery of our enemy, that they could not be frightened or deterred from attacking us, the governor ordered his men to fall back. . . ."

Rodriguez wrote: "The Escanjaques attacked noisily and shot numerous arrows, while the Spaniards fired their harquebuses and an artillery piece; after the latter had knocked down and killed a few Indians, the natives retired behind some rocks where they entrenched themselves and came out from time to time to shoot many arrows and set fire to the plain. This skirmish lasted four or five hours, and thirty soldiers received light wounds. We captured a few women, eight or ten boys, and a man. . . . That night the governor camped one-fourth of a league from the place where the fight occurred, keeping watch throughout the night. He ordered the women released. . . ."

The Oñate account went: "The governor stopped the battle to avoid further harm, retaining only a few boys, at the request of the friars, to teach them our holy Catholic faith, and also an Indian that he might furnish information about this land.

". . . We returned to our camp to spend the night. After dressing our wounds, we started out on the following day with our customary care. . . ."

Besides the aid of the Lord, the Spaniards had been blessed with a large measure of good luck. The Escanjaques, for some reason known only to themselves, chose not to pursue them. Oñate and his soldiers passed through the country of the Indians whom they called Vaqueros without further trouble, reaching San Gabriel on November 24. The snow was deep on the heights above the valley of the Rio Grande.

Oñate's disappointment was profound. He would make no further attempt to discover treasure in the region to which Coronado had given the name of Quivira, for he was convinced that none existed there, and his hope of finding a route to the North Sea had been shattered. The expedition had accomplished nothing. He had come perilously close to suffering the fate of the Humana company.

But it was not in his character to admit that he had failed, and in the report sent to the Viceroy his journey was termed a great triumph, and, swearing under oath that he was being truthful, he registered the opinion that more than two hundred thousand Indians dwelt in the High Plains over which he had traveled, and "considering the nature of the land" wagons could go easily to the North Sea, "which cannot be very far away" from the country of the Escanjaques, "because some Indians carried on their foreheads shells that had been brought from there.

"God our Lord be blessed for it all," he told the Viceroy. "May He hasten relief for these many souls, take pity on this land, and spread His holy gospel so that many poor people may find relief there, because from what we have seen it should be a refuge and a source of wealth for many."

4

Fray Alonso de Benavides would write in a report—he called it a *memorial*—that "without exaggeration, the huge Apache nation alone has more people than all the nations of New Spain, even including the Mexican." This, of course, was an absurd statement. Having been a missionary in the New World for more than three decades, and for eight years holder of the high office of Father Custodian in Santa Fe, he knew very well that the Indian population of Mexico was at least fifty times greater than that of New Mexico and Arizona. In another extravagant assertion, he declared that the country inhabited by the Apache extended from the buffalo plains of Texas, one hundred leagues east of the New Mexico mountains, "to the west as far as the South Sea [Pacific] . . . and continues up to the north, without our having found the end in that direction, and hits the Strait of Anian."

The memorial was prepared for the purpose of providing the Spanish king with accounts and descriptions of the tribes dwelling in New Mexico and informing him of conditions and problems existing there. Published in 1630, it made Benavides famous. Besides the monarch, his readers were the highest officials of the Church, ministers of state, and members of the Council of the Indies, and they were thrilled by the dramatic accounts of his perilous experiences and the triumphs of the apostles of Christianity among the savages of Spain's most inaccessible dominion.

Although valuable in many respects to scientists, the memorial has all the elasticity of a propaganda document. But if a historian is shocked by the rash claims Benavides knowingly and deliberately made, his reasons for making them are abundantly clear. He was campaigning to have more priests and more church funds sent to New Mexico, and to give the strongest possible support to his pleas he consistently overstated the number of Indians to be converted and the number of areas and settlements in dire need of missions and resident padres. He was envisioning a time when all lost souls in the colony would be saved, all satanic forces annihilated. And, obviously, if no one could delineate the boundaries of New Mexico, no one in Seville and Mexico City and Rome, not even the King or the Viceroy or the Pope, could profess to know how many Indians inhabited it.

During his tenure in New Mexico, Benavides had traveled extensively, both to carry out his business duties and to minister, on some journeys visiting the most remote missions of the province. In 1629 he was giving thought to returning to Mexico City, where he had been ordained as a young priest, and, as he said, "to finish my days there if He will allow me to do so." He was profoundly grieved by the fact that in the thirty years elapsing since the founding of the colony, all attempts to win converts among the Apache had been unsuccessful. He might have placed the blame for this situation, as many missionaries did, entirely on the corrupt practices of civil officials, but, being as practical as he was dedicated, he studiously sought to avoid administrative conflicts, recognizing their destructiveness. While he was at times severely critical of the governors, he also invoked the mitigating circumstance that the Apache were heathens manifestly unwilling to redeem themselves through spiritual regeneration.

Although a tragic event that took place in 1627 had brought him to the brink of utter discouragement, he, nevertheless, had stubbornly refused to concede that the resistance of the Apache to divine guidance was insuperable. In the fall of that year, with the hope that they might be able to establish a peaceful trade in the Spanish capital, a large band of Lipan had appeared in Santa Fe with a long packtrain of buffalo robes and other tanned hides. Some of them had wandered into a chapel on the plaza, and much to the delight of Benavides and other padres had expressed admiration of some religious paintings and a statue of the Virgin. Perhaps their interest was more diplomatic than genuine— they were shrewd salesmen and traders—but if Benavides saw that stone he left it unturned. Then "the demon had recourse to one of his wiles, choosing as his instrument the greed of our Spanish governor."

Most of the visiting Plains Apache were strong, young warriors who would have brought a high price from some mineowner in Mexico, and Governor Felipe Zotylo could not resist the temptation that obscured an opportunity for trade relations that would have been exceedingly profitable to him during his term in office. Under cover of darkness, he sent soldiers and Pueblo mercenaries to take the Plains Apache as his prisoners. In the fighting several raiders were mortally wounded by arrows, a score of the Plains Apache were killed, and perhaps twice that number, one a chieftain, were captured.

Benavides and other priests registered such vehement protests, charging Zotylo with making an unprovoked attack on Indians who had displayed a willingness to learn something of the Catholic faith, that he deemed it wise to release the prisoners he intended to sell into slavery. Benavides publicly condemned him, threatening to inform the Viceroy of his treachery, clearly an illegal act, and declaring that it would cause a revolt throughout the province.

It would do more than that. The liberated Plains Apache traders, leaving their dead and all their goods behind them, sped eastward to the safety of the plains beyond the Rio Pecos. The year had not ended when, for the first time, the Plains Apache issued a formal declaration of war, sending word throughout the southwest that they would wage an unrelenting offensive against the conquerors of New Mexico.

They would make good on their threat. Although during the century ahead the conflict would be marked with periods of quiet, during which the Plains Apache would curtail their aggressions, the peaceful intervals would be deceptive in appearance. If the fire of revenge burning in Plains Apache blood occasionally was reduced to smoldering, it would never be extinguished.

Benavides called the Plains Apache Vaqueros, and he told the King: "All this nation sustains itself on cows [buffalo]. Their meat is more savory and healthful than our cows, and the tallow much better. These cattle alone were enough to make a prince very powerful, if there could be, or might offer, a plan whereby they might be brought out to other lands. As these cattle are so many, and shed or change their hair every year, that wool remains in the fields, and the airs keep drifting it up to trees, or into sundry ravines, and in such quantity that it could make many rich, and it is all lost.[1]

Benavides wrote that in hunting buffalo the Plains Apache "go craftily to their watering places, and hide themselves in the trails, painted with red lead, and stained with mud, and when the cattle pass they employ the arrows which they carry.

"And afterward the Indians skin them and carry off the hide, the tongues, and tenderloins, and the sinews to sew with and to make strings for their bows. The hides they tan in two ways; some leave the hair on them, and they remain like a plush velvet, and serve as bed and cloak. Others they tan without hair, and thin them down.

"And with these hides they trade throughout all the land and gain their living. And it is the general dress as well among Indians [Pueblos] as Spaniards, who use it as well for service as bags, tents, cuirasses, shoes, and everything that is needed. When these Indians go to trade and traffic, the entire rancherias go, with their wives and children."

Benavides had good reasons for describing the Apache as a "people very fiery and bellicose, and very crafty in war. They have no more idolatry than that of the Sun, and even that is not general to all of them; and they scoff much at the other nations which have idols. They are wont to have as many wives as they can support; and upon her whom they find in adultery they irremissibly execute their law, which is to cut off her ears and nose; and they repudiate her.[2] They are very obedient to their elders and superiors and hold them in great respect. They pride themselves much on speaking the truth, and hold for dishonored him whom they catch in a lie." He was correct in his assertion that the Apache were "the crucible for the courage of the Spaniards," but incredible was his affirmation that they held the Spanish in high esteem and that they had told him that only Spaniards "merit the title of people, and that the nations of settled Indians do not."

As the time drew near when he would leave New Mexico forever, Benavides became determined to make a final attempt to fulfill a hope he had long held. It was to find an Apache chieftain whom he could convert and send back to his people to give light to the unholy darkness in which they dwelt. His efforts had been unsuccessful, and when he went in the fall of 1629 to minister temporarily at Santa Clara, a

Tewa pueblo on the upper Rio Grande and close to the country inhabited by the Jicarilla Apache, he decided to ask for assistance from the leaders of the parish.

After he had revealed his desire and had explained its purpose, twelve Tewa men volunteered to act as his emissaries and attempt to persuade an Apache "captain" to return with them to Santa Clara. "God knoweth," wrote Benavides, "the constriction in which my heart was, seeing the manifest risk in which I was putting those Indians."

It was a dramatic, if somewhat unbelievable, tale that Benavides told about this venture. According to it, the Tewa moved cautiously into the territory of "that untamed and ferocious nation, and when in sight of a rancheria signaled that they came in peace with important news. Told that they might safely proceed, they went drawing nearer, although slowly and with mistrust." An Apache chieftain came forward and they delivered Benavides's message and presented him with a packet of tobacco and a rosary. Having never seen a rosary, the Apache "asked what it signified that the thread had so many beads." It meant, said the Tewa spokesman, that Fray Benavides was "sending word that he would be his friend." Putting the rosary about his neck, the Apache declared that he welcomed peace, but it was apparent to the Tewas that "he was suspicious that they might have some double dealing." In the end, however, the Apache announced that he and three warriors would go to meet Benavides at Santa Clara.

The episode provides a noteworthy illustration of the haughtiness and boldness of these Plains Apache. They were undoubtedly Jicarilla, whom the Tewas easily could have reached by going up the Rio Grande to the vicinity of Taos. Despite the perilous situation, a chieftain—Benavides does not supply his Indian name—dared to go with only three companions to a pueblo that had been subdued and was controlled by Spaniards. One may only wonder why they took the chance, for they had no assurance that they would not be killed or captured and sent into slavery except the verbal promise of a padre that they would not be harmed— not to be depended upon under the prevailing conditions.

Benavides was excited and overjoyed, and he gathered "one thousand five hundred souls" to welcome the important guests. In order to assemble a throng of this size he would have been obliged to draw them from several pueblos, for the population of Santa Clara was no more than three hundred. The little Santa Clara church was suitably decorated, and "next to the altar I ordered a chair set upon a rug." Seated there he received the Apache. Solemn and impressive ceremonies followed. A Pueblo Indian presented his bow and arrows to the Apache chieftain, declaring that "before God, who was on that altar, he gave those weapons in earnest of his word that he would never break the peace." Not to be outdone, the Apache proffered one of his own arrows with the pledge "to that God, whoever he may be, I likewise give my word and faith, in the name of all my people, and that for my part and that of my people the peace and friendship shall never fail." Bells were rung, trumpets were sounded, and hymns were sung, to everyone's delight.

However, some dissension soon arose. The Apache declared that although he was trying hard, he was unable to find any sign of the God that he had been told was on the altar. Benavides' explanation that God would not be visible to him until he had been baptized was unsatisfactory, and he retorted that he "already took himself for a Christian," therefore "he also wished to see Him." A long argument followed, during which the Apache's belligerency increased, and at last Benavides ordered him to leave the church with the excuse that he wished to sing mass. The Apache and his companions stamped out in high dudgeon, and even after a good meal and perhaps a few drinks of Santa Clara firewa-

ter, their tempers somewhat cooled, the chieftain remained
"very vexed, because he wished to have seen God in the
mass." He demanded to know Benavides's name, and when
he was told that it was Alonso, "he said that I should give
him permission to be named so. I told him that he should
be named when he should be baptized." But the Apache saw
no reason to delay the matter, and in an overbearing
manner announced that he would take the name, and "from
that moment the Tewas all called him Don Alonso."

Upon departing for his home the Apache promised to
return in a few weeks with a large number of his people and
many gifts "to make a big fair," and that thenceforth peace
would exist between the Apache and the Spaniards, "and so
it was."

But, so it was not. Although he was well apprised of the
fact, Benavides did not trouble to tell his readers that no
Apache, no matter how high his rank, could speak for all
Apache or even for all the people of his own division. No
Apache possessed the authority to negotiate single-handedly
any type of agreement. Like many western Indian tribes, the
Apache maintained an almost pure democracy. Except on
military campaigns and raids for plunder, decisions reached
in public councils ruled them, not authoritarian chiefs.
There was no supreme governing body. Exigencies of the
moment influenced policies, and each group or division had
the right to act independently of all others.

The Apache "Alonso" knew that the pledges he made
were meaningless, for they were open to rejection by his
own people, as well as other bands. He understood that
there was no hope of peace between the Apache and Spanish. It is possible that for more than any other reason he had
gone to Santa Clara to spy. Yet he had been no more deceit-
ful or hypocritical than his host. Benavides could not have
been unaware of the futility of the show he staged. Unques-
tionably it bolstered his ego and gave him spiritual satisfac-

tion, but he fully understood that no effort he made could bridge the chasm that his own people, falsely acting in the name of God, had created between the Spanish and Apache worlds.

And so it would be until other forces had ended the conflict between the Plains Apache and the Spanish in New Mexico.

5

Trade, especially that carried on between the Plains Apache and the Pueblos, was the foundation of the Indian economy in the province of New Mexico. This commerce, molded in a primitive structure, was a bridge over which passed the products of regions vastly in contrast with each other. Their differences were not only in physical geography, climate, indigenous vegetation, and animals, but in the characters and the cultures of the people inhabiting them. These components were the bases from which grew demands and desires, and they were the sources of the urges that led to inventive productivity.

Every Pueblo Indian, from the Jemez of Pecos to the Hopi of Arizona, wanted the robes and tanned skins, the tallow and fat, the jerky and pemmican, and the horns and hair that came from the buffalo. Yet, buffalo were not to be found in their arid land.

Every Plains Apache, from the Lipans of southern Texas to the Gattackas of Nebraska, wanted the corn and dried calabashes and beans, the mineral cosmetics and dyes, the cotton weavings, the Pacific shells, the turquoises and other bright stones, and the ceramic ornaments and utensils that the Pueblos possessed. And such things were not to be found on their plains.

It was an ancient commerce, moving over its wilderness routes for centuries before white men knew it existed. On the High Plains the bones of *Bison bison occidentalis*—the modern buffalo—slaughtered nine thousand years ago by human hunters have been discovered. Maize was being grown in New Mexico in B.C. 4000, for ancient ears of corn from that era have been found in dry caves. The minerals and bright stones were put there when the earth forms, as man found them, were created.

From the time of colonization, blinded by greed and religious bigotry and enmeshed in a jumble of royal decrees, the Spanish systematically disrupted and destroyed the only means by which their own economic stability might have been achieved. Political appointees and priests fought each other, not infrequently descending to confiscation, thievery, undisguised corruption, and incredibly brutal practices, to gain control of supply channels and monopolies of all commodities that were marketable in Mexico, the West Indies, and Spain.

Governors levied tributes that kept the Pueblos in a state of abject poverty. Both high government officials and ranking missionaries maintained *encomiendas* in which Indian workers, held in bondage, received nothing in reward for their labors but some rags to wear, crumbling adobes to live in, barely enough food to keep them alive, and broken bodies.

The Spanish wanted the fine robes and leather products the Plains Apache made, but they wanted another commodity even more. It came in human form. There were great difficulties in capturing slaves. Because of their nomadism and their wide distribution, the Plains Apache were not easily controlled, and expenses involved in attempts to cap-

ture them usually left little margin for profit. But the Santa
Fe government could see no alternative to their forceful
methods to achieve the end desired. Less than a third of the
seventeenth century had elapsed before all trade between
the Plains Apache and the valley of the Rio Grande was
restricted to such an extent that it could be carried on only
in outlying areas, in such places as Taos and Pecos and a few
smaller Indian settlements on the eastern perimeter of the
province.

There were laws designed to resolve such problems. Spe-
cifically they decreed that only Indians taken prisoner in
open warfare, heathens, and cannibals were subject to
enslavement. The statutes could hardly be termed handicaps
for anyone engaging in the vicious trade; indeed, they were
so easily circumvented that enforcing them was practically
impossible.

It was easy to start a war. All slave hunters had to do was
to confiscate Indian property, shoot an old man or two, or
fire a village, and any retaliation by the victims could be
termed an act of war. It was not even necessary to commit
such atrocities against the Plains Apache, for, unlike the
helpless Pueblos, they had not capitulated to Spanish
power, had not sworn allegiance to the Spanish king or to
the Spanish church. Thus, they were wild, heathen Indians,
and under this designation could be legally enslaved. But
the officials who conducted raids against the Plains Apache
for the purpose of taking captives sought to provide greater
justification for their own acts by reporting that they were
cannibals and were carrying off Christianized Pueblos to
cook and eat them.

With only two or three minor exceptions, the Plains
Apache, beginning at the time of Coronado, had sought to
maintain peaceful relations with the Spanish. Disruptions of
their commerce and swindling by traders and officials were
injustices which, though deeply resented and remembered,

they could accept without resorting to violent retaliation. But wanton murders and enslavement aroused in them an uncontrollable passion for vengeance.

However, this was not a new emotion; indeed, it was very old, for it had always been as much a part of intertribal warfare as bloodshed. Traditionally, men, women, and children taken by a tribe in combat were spoils which the tribe might exchange for its own people held by an ememy or for property it had lost to raiders. When these courses were closed, a tribe might—and all of them often did—dispose of unwanted captives by fiendish tortures or simply by cutting off their heads.

With the advent of the Spanish, the situation rapidly changed. The establishment of settlements, *presidios*, missions, and *encomiendas* not only increased the slaughter and the traffic in human beings within the colony, but also opened permanent connections with slave dealers in Mexico. A condition was created that was far more perilous than that with which the tribes had been forced to contend in prehistoric years.

The time came, between 1640 and 1650, when the Plains Apache would attempt to foment a Pueblo uprising, and would offer to unite with those Indians in attacking Spanish supply trains, missions, and ranches. This policy combined retaliation and aggression, and was generated by endogenous compulsion, defiance, pride, and sheer necessity. Putting it into operation had been delayed by a deficiency of certain resources, namely guns and horses. There was no possibility of obtaining the desirable quantity of firearms, but acquiring mobility was much less of a problem. The facility for striking unexpectedly and retreating rapidly to safe havens inaugurated an era of cooperation in guerrilla tactics. While the decision to act in concert was made independently by the many groups and bands—there was no representative government with the power to command adoption of any plan—nevertheless, it was a decision that united the Plains Apache both politically and militarily to a degree that was without precedent.

The Pueblos, an enslaved people, had nothing to contribute to an amalgamation, nothing except their own hatred and hopes and the strength of their bodies. Hundreds of them slipped away from the *encomiendas* and the mission factories and found refuge among the Navajo and both the Plains and the Western Apache in southern New Mexico and Arizona. Occasionally some of them mustered up enough courage to revolt, and paid for their defiance with their lives. In an uprising in 1639, the Taos killed several soldiers and priests, and before the inevitable Spanish retaliation came they abandoned their pueblos and fled to their friends, the Plains Apache in southeastern Colorado and western Kansas. They were welcomed, not because they were allies but also because they brought with them a large herd of stolen horses. In the region called El Cuartelejo the Taos built new towns. They would occupy them for a number of years before the Spanish military was able to force them to return to their ancient dwellings near the Rio Grande.

But not only the destitution of the Pueblos was responsible for the failure of the Plains Apache plan. The main cause was the divisiveness that existed, and had always existed, among the Pueblos themselves. The independence so greatly valued by each tribe, even by each group within a tribe, their pride in bloodlines, their unwillingness to share the perils and sufferings that would be unavoidable in fighting a common foe, their inability to organize, their deeply rooted jealousies, their constant attempts to take booty from each other, and their eternal imaginary feuds all contributed to their internal division.

Even when, at last, leaders would arise who were influential enough to organize a military alliance among the Pueblos, distrust and ego and personal ambitions gnawed at the frail foundation on which it had been constructed until it disintegrated. The great Pueblo revolt of 1680 would drive the Spanish from New Mexico, but no sooner had they gone than Pueblo tribes were once again acting independently, each withdrawing into its own little world. Even though the will to continue fighting the Spanish remained undiminished in most of them, there would be little cohesion in future defensive actions.

The operations of the Plains Apache were not affected as much by tribal divisiveness as by their nomadic life-style. They roamed over an enormous region, bands separated by hundreds of miles, and cooperation was seldom feasible. Yet, when the Spanish did return to New Mexico they would encounter a Plains Apache front reaching from the Rio Grande in Texas to the Rio Platte in Nebraska. All the tribes along it, whether acting independently or in unison, were determined to defend their own homeland and to preserve their individual freedom.

The governorship of New Mexico and the task of reconquering the province had been awarded by King Carlos II in 1690 to Diego de Vargas Zapata Luján Ponce de León, an extremely wealthy man with an illustrious record as a soldier and diplomat, and the scion of a great family whose members for generations had won renown in serving both the state and the church. Vargas was sworn into office in 1691 but was prevented from starting for Santa Fe for more than a year by orders to conduct a campaign against the Western Apache, who were ravaging the northern states of Mexico.

By the summer of 1692, the Western Apache were far from being defeated, but there were urgent reasons why the reconquest of New Mexico could no longer be delayed. The French had gained control of the Mississippi Valley. *Voyageurs* were reported pushing westward across both the

southern and northern Great Plains. The boundaries of
New Mexico remained officially undefined; indeed, it was
still unknown how far the continent extended to the north.
Under such circumstances, Spain's claims might be open to
dispute, perhaps by Russia and Great Britain, as well as by
France. Moreover, with the Indians in control of New
Mexico, Mexico was without an adequate buffer zone on the
north to protect it from an invasion by any European power
from that direction. There was another reason why no further postponements of the reconquest could be tolerated: It
had to do with pride and religion. For the first and only
time in the New World, a horde of savages not only had successfully defied the military strength of Spain but also had
profaned for twelve years the only true faith.

Vargas started north from El Paso del Norte in August.
Reinforcements and supplies reportedly were en route to
him, but he did not wait for them. He set out on the trail
up the Rio Grande with only sixty regular cavalrymen, a
hundred Indian auxiliaries, and three padres. Strangely he
was not harassed by the Plains Apache, and the pueblos
along the route were deserted.

The reconquest of New Mexico is not properly within the
scope of this work. The Plains Apache made no attempt to
stand in the way of the Spanish offensive. And, except for
skirting its western perimeter, Vargas did not enter the
country, nor did he attempt at once to open negotiations
with the Apache. The Pueblos fought bravely, and
hundreds of them were slain—all but four occupied pueblos
had to be taken by assault—but Vargas, his forces steadily
augmented by troops from El Paso, swept through the land
waging a relentless campaign in summer and winter until,
by the end of 1693, New Mexico was once again a Spanish
province.

The Plains Apache continued to stay out of the way.
They slipped into Pecos and Taos and a few other moun-

tain settlements to barter their products—probably nothing could have prevented them from surreptitiously conducting trade whenever possible—and slipped away again into the vastness of their grass domain.

But suddenly, in the summer of 1695, they struck. Joining several groups of northern Pueblos who had refused to capitulate and had concealed themselves in remote areas, they swept from the north down the valley of the Rio Grande. Most Spaniards fled before them to Santa Fe, but within a few days twenty-one soldiers, five priests, and a number of civilian colonists had been slain, three churches had been destroyed, and several hundred horses and mules had been stolen.

Vargas moved fast. Some of the Pueblo rebels were captured and executed. But the hunt was largely unsuccessful until, in October, Vargas was informed that Plains Apache were aiding a large group to escape to northeastern New Mexico with all their possessions and a number of horses and other livestock stolen from Spanish ranchos. With a contingent of cavalrymen and Indian guides he set out in swift pursuit. He found Picuris Pueblo deserted, but, not far beyond, his scouts picked up the trail of the fugitives, who were forced to travel slowly because of their heavy loads and the big band of sheep and goats they had with them.

As he pressed on, Vargas found the trail littered with discarded tipi skins, household utensils, and other articles, leaving no doubt that the runaways were aware that he was after them. The weather turned cold and snow fell, but Vargas did not stop. Some of the Picuris and Taos were overtaken huddled together in a ravine, and during the next two days others, having given up hope of escaping, came into the Spanish camp.

No Plains Apache had been encountered, but their campsites had been found, and the scouts reported that they were not far ahead. Deep snow and high winds prevented Vargas from continuing. Some animals froze to death, and their meat was fed to the captives, who numbered eighty-four, among them several suckling babes. When he reached Santa Fe, Vargas gave all the prisoners as slaves to the soldiers and scouts who had accompanied him. He was profoundly aggravated by the fact that many of his quarry, aided by Plains Apache, had eluded him. The greatest prize of all, Lorenzo, chief of the Picuris, had gotten away.

The brief winter sally of Vargas—the first to enter northeastern New Mexico in two decades—had harmed the Plains Apache not at all, but they regarded it as a forewarning of perils to come. The Spanish obviously intended to make every effort to confine the Pueblos in the stronghold of New Mexico, but, more than that, it was clear that they would not hesitate to extend their military incursions beyond the mountains east of the Rio Grande—to the High Plains.

But the Plains Apache would soon understand that enemies even stronger and more deadly—and certainly more efficient—than the Spanish lurked on the northern horizon.

PART FIVE

Turmoil

1

A few years before the Pueblo revolt of 1680, strange Indians who, in time, the Spanish would call *Yutas*, began to filter down from the north into the rugged high country between the upper Rio Grande and the valley of the Rio San Juan. The Spanish would be driven out of New Mexico before they had a chance to learn much, if anything, about them, but after the reconquest of the province in 1692 they would know them very well.

The Yutas were the Ute, a branch of the Shoshonean linguistic family, and their homeland was in the vast arid territory that now comprises western Colorado and eastern Utah. They drifted southward in very small groups at first, poor and on foot, drawn by the wonders of Spanish civilization, seeking to ingratiate themselves with the more affluent Navajo and Plains Apache, and for a time, until their true objectives were revealed, they were successful, intermarrying with these tribes and enjoying the benefits of their raids on pueblos, Spanish settlements, and missions.

The number of Ute bands migrating southward steadily increased, and before the end of the Pueblo uprising they

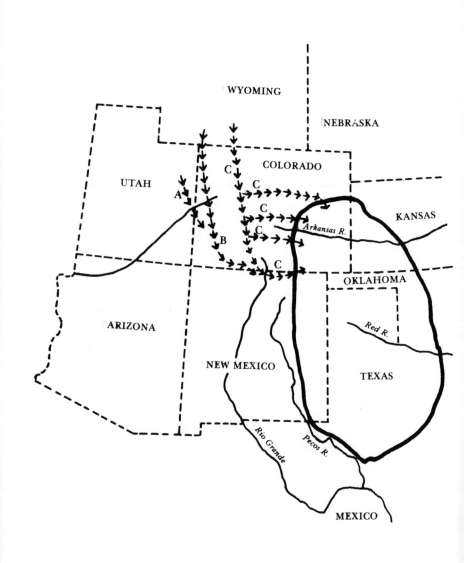

WYOMING

NEBRASKA

UTAH

COLORADO

C

C

C

C

C

Arkansas R.

KANSAS

A

B

C

OKLAHOMA

ARIZONA

Red R.

NEW MEXICO

TEXAS

Rio Grande

Pecos R.

MEXICO

Invasion of Plains Apache Territory by
Shoshoni, Ute, and Comanche

A. Ute, c. 1670
B. Comanche and Ute, c. 1700
C. Comanche, c. 1702–1725

Approximate territory held by the Comanche after
conquering the Plains Apache in the
eighteenth century

Scale: 1 inch is approximately 225 miles

had acquired enough horses and metal weapons, such as knives, swords, and lances, to operate attacking forces of their own. They not only raided the northern pueblos but they also turned on their former friends, striking the Navajo west of Jemez and the Apache on the High Plains in north-eastern New Mexico and eastern Colorado. When the Spanish returned in 1692 they found, besides the Navajo and the Plains Apache, a third wild tribe to contend with north of Taos. And by the beginning of the eighteenth century there was a fourth.

According to historian George E. Hyde,[1] "It was about the year 1700 that the Utes brought the first group of their Comanche kinsmen into New Mexico, to visit Taos, and from that time the Comanches joined the Utes in their raiding operations. They raided the Navajos and the Pueblos, then shifted their attention to the Apache in the Colorado plains and began to raid them."

The Comanche,[2] who also spoke the Shoshonean tongue, lived north of the Ute, their range at the beginning of historical times encompassing northwestern Colorado and a large part of Wyoming. Probably only a relatively small number of them moved south to join the Ute on raids into New Mexico, but the successes on these forays, modest as they may have been at first, created an insatiable desire for horses and a consuming ambition to gain the military power and the prosperity that it could bring them. There was only one way to achieve those ends: the development of brigandage matchless in its efficiency.

The economic conflict that raged through the first four decades of the eighteenth century between the Comanche and the Plains Apache cannot be compared in destructiveness and in constancy with any other confrontation in Indian history. Human qualities of courage, physical stamina, intelligence, and tenacity were not the criteria that determined its outcome, for in these respects neither antagonist was superior to the other. It was a combination of other factors and circumstances that created pressures the Plains Apache could not withstand.

The Comanche gradually broke away from the Ute, devising their own campaigns. There were a number of mountain passes, easily reached from their homeland, through which they could travel to the High Plains, bringing them into the vicinity of the contemporary cities of Denver, Colorado Springs, and Pueblo. They struck at the Plains Apache from these areas, moving along the eastern front of the mountains, into which they could flee with their spoils. By this route they continued southward into southeastern Colorado and northeastern New Mexico, where there were numerous bands of Plains Apache.

During the latter years of the seventeenth century, and perhaps a decade or two earlier, the Plains Apache of the El Cuartelejo region and along the Canadian River and its tributaries in northeastern New Mexico had begun to engage in agriculture on a small scale. They established permanent rancherias in places where dependable water for irrigation was available or where the rainfall was normally sufficient, and they planted little patches of maize, beans, and squashes in the spring. They would spend the summers hunting in their customary way, following the herds on the plains. After harvesting the crops and storing them they would resume their nomadic life once more. They would never become dedicated farmers, and their production of domesticated vegetables would never offset the need to trade for these commodities. Yet even these insignificant attempts to change their culture by adopting practices of sedentary Indians, whom they had always held in contempt, contributed adversely to their welfare. They made the mistake of acquiring property and possessions.

The Utes and Comanches soon came to know that they would find these Apache who dabbled in horticulture at their rancherias in the spring and in late summer. The strategy of the raiders, striking both from the west and from the north, as Hyde points out, was "to catch the Apache off guard at their rancherias, to make a sudden assault, kill as many Apache as they could, capture some women and children for the slave trade . . . and plunder the rancherias and destroy the huts and crops. Thus, with each succeeding attack the Utes and Comanches grew stronger, the Apache weaker and more alarmed." The attackers, in every raid, "swept off all the Apache horses they could get at, leaving their victims without mounts, and thus without the means of making effective summer and winter buffalo hunts, from which they still derived their principal support."

By 1710 the Plains Apache, notably the Gattacka and the Padouca, apparently had halted their long-distance raids against the Caddoans and other tribes that dwelt several hundred miles to the east of them. This was a transition of paramount importance. For in the past, strong forces of Plains Apache, at first traveling on foot with dog packtrains, and later on with horses, had conducted raids into eastern Nebraska and Kansas, far down the Arkansas and Red Rivers in Oklahoma and Texas, slaughtered hundreds of Indians of the southern Great Plains, plundering tribes with such devastating effect that many of them were forced to flee their homelands or to band together for mutual defense. The westward advance of French traders, who supplied the Caddoans, Pawnee, Kansa, and other people with guns and ammunition in exchange for furs and Indian captives for the slave trade, was one of two reasons why the Plains Apache were forced to cease their eastern forays. The other, of course, was the steadily increasing number of invasions by the Shoshoneans, forcing them to defend themselves in their own country.

But the Plains Apache did not halt their raiding altogether—far from it. They gave their attention instead to Spanish settlements. The Lipan, Natagee, Teya, and other bands swept far south into Texas. The Faraon struck in the Galisteo Basin and in the valley of the Rio Grande. In both regions Spanish colonists were murdered in their fields and in their beds, buildings were burned, trade caravans were attacked, and herds of horses were stolen. Punitive expeditions sent against them had little effect, but they drew the attention of the Spanish military away from other raiders on the northern frontier, and no help was sent to the more peaceable Jicarilla and other groups who were suffering from Ute and Comanche incursions.

The presence of the French as they pushed westward toward New Mexico had become more apparent with the passage of each year. As early as 1695 some Chipayne Apache visiting Picuris Pueblo declared that white men from the east had attacked a band of Conejeros in western Kansas. In 1696 a Jicarilla had reported to Spanish authorities that a French company was approaching El Cuartelejo. In the same year two Plains Apache chiefs visiting in Taos said that all Apache tribes along the Canadian River had been informed that white men were in Quivira.

Shortly, more alarming news reached New Mexico, this time purportedly disseminated by the Navajo. In 1697, states Alfred B. Thomas, a leading authority on Spanish history in the southwest, ". . . the Navajo made another of their customary expeditions to the east. The French and Pawnee, however, destroyed, so it was reported, four thousand of the invaders. In 1698 the Navajos returned for vengeance and annihilated three Pawnee rancherias and a fortified place. Returning in 1699, they appeared at the Spanish fair laden with spoil: slaves, jewels, carbines, cannons, powder flasks, *gamellas*, sword belts, waistcoats, shoes, and even small pots of brass. They then related to the aston-

ished Spaniards the defeat of the year before and praised the
French for their valor, their dexterity in shooting, and their
readiness in reinforcing their allies."[3]

It is very doubtful that these raiders were Navajo. Some
scholars think they were Plains Apache, a view in which this
author concurs. Equally open to question is the report on
the number of casualties. The assertion that four thousand
invaders, either Navajo or Plains Apache, were slain in an
attack on Pawnee villages in the middle Great Plains is in
itself patently absurd. Indeed, there is no reliable evidence
even suggesting that a Navajo or Plains Apache force of
such size ever participated in a single raid against any Caddoan tribe. Four hundred would be a more believable
figure.

Nevertheless, whether these raiders were Apache or
Navajo their accounts and the booty they displayed made it
unquestionable that they had engaged French traders. And
Spanish concern was augmented by reports that Frenchmen
and unidentified Indians had destroyed a Jumano band in
western Texas and that a white man, presumably a Frenchman, had been slain by Indians from Pecos who were hunting east of the river bearing that name.

While New Mexico's governor, Francisco Cuervo y
Valdez, was profoundly apprehensive, it was not only the
incidents involving the French that brought him to the decision to send a military expedition northeast to El Cuartelejo. He had received a message from the refugee chief of
the Picuris Pueblos, Lorenzo, informing him that Indians of
that area were suffering greatly under attacks by the Comanche. Besides asking for assistance from the Spanish, Lorenzo
prayed for forgiveness and asked for permission to lead the
Picuris runaways back to their ancient home on the Rio
Grande.

Governor Cuervo looked upon the appeal as an opportunity to bring the Picuris back under Spanish control, and, as

he would write the Viceroy, the Duke of Albuquerque, to rescue them from a life as apostates under the barbarous oppression of Apache infidels and Satan. If God favored him, he might also be able to establish an alliance with El Cuartelejo Apache bands, thereby strengthening defenses on the north. In addition to these desirable accomplishments, there was the possibility that an expedition might obtain reliable intelligence as to the whereabouts and the activities of the French.

In a council at Santa Fe, Captain Juan de Ulibarri was chosen to undertake the mission, and these objectives were assigned to him. He was also ordered to make a show of force before any Indians he encountered and warn them that further attacks on Spanish settlements would be followed with a campaign to annihilate them.

2

Captain Ulibarri started from Santa Fe on July 13, 1706, taking the road that ran northward in the Rio Grande Valley to Taos. Only twenty-eight professional soldiers were assigned to accompany him, an illustration of the paucity of the province's military strength. The balance of his force—all of which was well equipped with reserve mounts and guns—was composed of one hundred men recruited from several pueblos; a priest, Fray Domingo de Aranz; a noted frontiersman, José Naranjo, serving as chief scout and guide; and twelve colonists of various callings who were experienced in Indian warfare.

Ironically, one of the civilians was a Frenchman, Juan de L'Archeveque, who had participated in the murder of La Salle in 1687. He had been captured by a Spanish military contingent in eastern Texas, where the slaying of the famous explorer had taken place, but eventually had been released and given permission to make his residence in Santa Fe and to become a trader. The killing of a man who had attempted to establish a French colony in Spanish territory had not been looked upon by authorities in Mexico City as a capital crime.

Ulibarri kept a diary which provides some valuable glimpses of the Plains Apache dwelling northeast of New Mexico at the time, and clearly denotes their fear of the Comanche.[1]

From Taos, Ulibarri followed the ancient trail over Palo Flechado Pass. After traveling two or three days through high mountains, the pleasant, well-watered country in the vicinity of the present Cimarron, New Mexico, was reached. Here Plains Apache of the Conejero, Acho, and Rio Colorados bands appeared, obviously having assembled to confer with him. According to Ulibarri, they told him that "all the tribes were very happy that we Spaniards were coming into their lands and among their rancherias without doing them any injury. But that it would be well to guard ourselves from other nations who were on the road in the distance, particularly from those called the Penxaye, Fleches de Palos, Limita, and Tremintina.[2] These had always been very bad thieves and had even injured them. I answered them that I esteemed very highly their information and advice, but that I was trusting in our God who was the creator of everything and who was to keep us free of the greatest dangers." He gave them some tobacco, knives, and other articles, after which "they went away satisfied."

It was clearly evident that not all the Plains Apache bands ranging through the region were on good terms with each other. The cause of this situation, as Ulibarri would soon learn, was the eagerness of each group to gain special favors from the Spanish in the form of measures that would aid it in protecting itself against raiders. The Plains Apache had no policies for their common good or mutual defense.

Going on northeast across the headwater tributaries of the Canadian River, Ulibarri found Jicarilla, Carlana, and more

Fleches de Palos tribesmen waiting for him. The council was identical to that held on Cimarron Creek. He wrote, "They showed a great deal of friendship toward us, saying they were coming to give me many manifestations of gratitude for having entered their land without doing them any injury; that they were all very happy; and that on my return I would find them together in the rancherias of the Jicarillas. There they would give me raisins which they always preserved for the most worthy Spaniards; that they were very good people; they had not stolen anything from anyone because they are busy with the sowing of corn, *frijoles*, and pumpkins." Ulibarri distributed small gifts among them, "and they went away very happy." So convinced was he that they could be trusted that he left a number of tired and weak horses in their care.

More Jicarilla were encountered the following day, and they demonstrated their friendship by warning him that Comanche were probably waiting to attack him in Raton Pass, which was on the customary route to El Cuartelejo. He rewarded them, and having no intention, despite his orders, of attempting to make a show of force to savages lying in ambush in a mountain defile, he turned sharply north.

Several Plains Apache he does not identify by a tribal name volunteered to act as guides, and they led him through rough high country on a trail that crossed the Purgatoire, Apishapa, and Huerfino Rivers. On the twenty-ninth of July they arrived "at the large river which all the tribes call the Napestle." It was the Arkansas River, and Ulibarri would be the first European to describe the river in this vicinity. He camped opposite the mouth of Fountain Creek, where the city of Pueblo, Colorado, would rise. Against the clear sky in the northwest a great blue pile could be seen, and more than a century later it would be unjustly given the name Pike's Peak.

Ulibarri said of the Arkansas, which he called Rio Grande de San Franciso in honor of Governor Francisco Cuervó, "It is much more than four times as large as the Rio del Norte [Rio Grande] and bathes the best and broadest valley discovered in New Spain. It has many poplar trees and throughout the upper part most beautiful stretches." He thought the plain along the river "extremely fertile as is shown by the many plums, cherries, and wild grapes which there are on it." Crossing the river took as long as "the equivalent of thirty-three Credos recited very slowly," a means of measuring distance unique if somewhat unscientific.

The company traveled up Fountain Creek for a few miles and then turned eastward, the Plains Apache guides informing Ulibarri that they were taking the most direct trail but that the march would be difficult because water holes were widely separated. The tilting plains were awesome in their immensity, Ulibarri recounting that the scouts took their direction "from hummocks of grass placed a short distance apart on the trail by the Apaches, who lose even themselves there. In this way they had marked out the course. All of this was of no use, for we became entirely lost." Evidently more Plains Apache joined the Spaniards, for he recorded that "the Indians, according to their shallow natures, were overcome with fear to such extreme despondency that they almost wept. I placed myself under the patronage of Our Lady the Virgin Mary, conqueress of this kingdom and of the Glorious Patriarch, San Ignacio de Loyola. . . . It was the good fortune that two scouts who searched the land found water very far above from where we were. The news of this filled the whole camp with joy, and many thanks were given to God and his most holy Mother because of whose good will I ordered that the spring be named El Ojo de Nuestra Senora del Buen Suceso. . . . Realizing that the animals were very badly tired out, I left eighteen mules and horses in this spot to pick up on the return, in spite of the contingency and risk that they might be carried off."

After the company was lost a second time and wandered helplessly for a day or two, scouts led them to a Plains Apache rancheria, the name of which Ulibarri set down as Tachichichi.³ Regrettably, he did not identify the band inhabiting it or provide any geographical clue as to its location. However, the place is worthy of note for two reasons:

Among the inhabitants were several Picuris, and one of them gave Ulibarri a message from Lorenzo, the Picuris chief. Lorenzo wanted him to know that "everyone is happy" knowing the Spaniards were there.

And it was in Tachichichi that a Plains Apache leader told Ulibarri that only four days earlier, near a large rancheria farther east "they had killed a white man. They had taken from him a large gun, a kettle, a red-lined cap, the powder which he carried. At the same time they had killed a woman who was going with this white man. From what they heard us say they now considered them French. The poor woman was pregnant; the hair was hers and not that of the man, who was bald." If Ulibarri would go to the rancheria they would show him the scalp and the spoils. Ulibarri wasted no time in accepting the offer.

Ulibarri apparently remained on a course some miles north of the Arkansas River, but how far eastward he traveled must remain a matter of speculation. The distances he recorded in leagues suggest that he may have traveled as far as the Colorado-Kansas boundary in the present Kiowa County. Some scholars think he went into western Kansas. The names he gave to streams and Plains Apache villages cannot be connected with place names of today.

However, he had extended Spanish military activities into country not previously penetrated by an official expedition, and at a place he called Ojo de Santa Rita he took possession of El Cuartelejo in the name of the Spanish king in an impressive ceremony.

Several hundred Plains Apache, including a number of chieftains, had gathered at Ojo de Santa Rita, which was located "in a very pleasant dale. . . . From out of the huts came Don Lorenzo and the rest of the Picuris Indians, men and women, who were with him. . . . They cried for joy."

The shrewdness of the El Cuartelejo Plains Apache in realizing how greatly the Spanish were influenced and guided by religious doctrines and customs was dramatically illustrated. Ulibarri gave vent to joy himself when he saw on a rise near Ojo de Santa Rita "a most holy cross which the Apaches had set up." And he would express in his diary the belief that they "are a people more inclined to our Catholic faith than any of all those that are thus reduced. Though heathens, the majority of the Apaches wear many crosses, medals, and rosaries around their necks. We knew they were very old because the crosses are covered with perspiration and the girdles or chamois bags in which they carry them are very grimy and have been repaired. We asked them the reasons they had for wearing crosses, medallions, and rosaries without knowing what they were. They replied that for many years they traded and had commerce with the Spaniards and they knew that because they [the Spaniards] wore crosses and rosaries and images of saints, that they are very valiant; that there is no nation that can conquer them, and that when the Apache fight with their enemies, and become tired, they remember the great Captain of the Spaniards who is in the heavens and then their weariness leaves them and they feel refreshed. They knelt down every night that they saw us on our knees worshipping the rosary of Our Lady the Virgin Mary, and other prayers. After this ceremony was finished, they did as the rest of the Spaniards and [Pueblo] Indians, which was to kiss the sleeve of the holy garment of the padre." If this passage suggests that a dangerous naíveté marked Ulibarri's character, it also demonstrates that he wanted fervently to believe what he saw and heard.

The gun taken from the white man was shown to Ulibarri by a Plains Apache chief, who changed the story as to how it had been acquired, apparently fearing that he would think it had been taken from a Spaniard. The weapon, declared the chief, had been captured in a fight with Pawnee raiders.

It should be noted that although they fully understood the value and the power of guns, most Indians of the time mistreated them and gave them no care at all. They used them as clubs, as digging tools, as tipi pegs, decorated them with studs, scalps, paint, and gewgaws, and took them apart, using the plates as hide scrapers. Had the gun displayed by the Apache chief showed signs of such abuse, it would have given Ulibarri less concern than it did, but it was still shiny, unbattered, and unbroken. If it had been obtained from the Pawnee, it had not been in their possession for any length of time.

Ulibarri settled the question by summoning the Frenchman, Juan de L'Archeveque, who, after carefully examining the gun, declared that it was a type manufactured by the French for trade with the Indians.

Ulibarri attributed the Plains Apache chief's refusal to produce the kettle, red-lined cap, "and other spoils" which it had been claimed were taken from the white man and the pregnant woman to his fear of reprisal.[4] Alarmed and angered by the turn of affairs, Ulibarri summoned Plains Apache leaders to a council and sternly warned them that they would suffer the force of Spanish arms if they deceived him or attempted in any manner to prevent him from performing his duties. A Plains Apache spokesman declared that his people were prepared to cooperate with the Spanish in every respect and to obey their commands, and then

countered with no little adroitness that Ulibarri could dem-
onstrate the proclaimed intention of the Spanish to befriend
El Cuartelejo Apache by "going with them to attack their
enemies, the Pawnee Indians, since it was only a seven days'
journey across level land with sufficient water."

Ulibarri's response to this proposal was "that another
occasion would not be lacking in which to aid them; at that
time I was determined only to bring back the Picuries. Further, I might lose the largest part of my horses, as their feet
had become very sore. Also, in order not to frighten them
[the Plains Apache] away, I had not brought with me a
bugle and a drum. Finally, it was very necessary for me to
return shortly because of the winter which was coming; and
that I would come another year in May or June and we
would succeed in helping them against their enemies."

The Apache negotiator accepted these excuses without
argument, but proffered another suggestion: Inasmuch as
the French were supplying the Pawnee with guns, couldn't
Ulibarri leave with them some of his guns—old ones would
do—to help them defend themselves? Ulibarri thought this
plan infeasible, but he left other articles with the Plains
Apache—food and clothing and trinkets—and he felt convinced that the Indians were pleased and satisfied.

Ulibarri took back with him Lorenzo and sixty-two
Picuris. When he reached the Jicarilla he learned that soon
after he had left them they had suffered from two raids by
Utes and Comanches, but, as they had promised they would
do, they had protected his horses, and the animals were
turned over to him. Early in September he reached Santa Fe
and made his report to Governor Cuervó.

The intelligence he had gathered about the French was
disappointing and inconclusive. The few spoils of French
manufacture found in the possession of the Plains Apache
and the alleged killing of a bald white man and a pregnant
white woman were hardly enough evidence to indicate that

an invasion of New Mexico by the French was imminent.
Yet the articles could be accepted as confirmation of the
presence of French traders among some tribes, and notably
the Pawnee, that dwelt in the Great Plains to the east of El
Cuartelejo.

If Governor Cuervó felt it was a situation worth watching, he was not sufficiently alarmed to mention it in the
report of Ulibarri's expedition that he sent to Mexico City.
Instead he gave precedence to the "rescue of the Picuries,"
writing the Viceroy, the Duke of Albuquerque, that all of
them had been absolved of their crime of running away, and
not forgetting to point out the great service he and Ulibarri
had rendered to the two majesties, God and the King, in
freeing the poor souls from the "apostasy in which they
were," and restoring them to "their original and ancient
pueblo, where they are quiet and content," a feat achieved
"with success and fortune, all at my cost and without
expense to the royal treasury."

3

The province of New Mexico and its vast unexplored environs remained vaguely defined, except on the south, in the first quarter of the eighteenth century, and comprised an immense theater seething in bloody warfare. From the Spanish standpoint the turmoil was not created entirely by incursions of hostile Indians, although defense against their attacks was by far the most persistently crucial problem harrying colonial governors. Turmoil was also caused by restrictive religious decrees, many of which were equal, if not superior, in judicial standing to criminal statutes.

Noting that the Spanish would never be completely buttressed against red raiders, Thomas declares that "it is to their credit that the Spanish pioneers never adopted the doubtful expedient of their Anglo-Saxon successors: extermination."[1] While no humane person would quarrel with that statement, several addenda should be affixed to it. The punishments inflicted by the Spanish on Indians who dared to defend themselves and their lands were inconceivably fiendish and monstrous. The objective of forcing them to accept Christianity was given priority above all other goals pronounced by the highest Spanish authorities, not excluding those goals set by a series of kings. For the doctrines of the Roman Catholic church were the walls and roof enclosing the social, economic, and legal beams of the Spanish monarchal structure. If the "expedient of extermination" had not been precluded by both ecclesiastical and royal edicts, military leaders would have resorted to it. And its combination with the circumvention of laws governing slavery would have resulted in the greater reduction of the southwestern Indians than that which did occur, perhaps their complete annihilation. Compassion was a quality as dormant in the Spanish character as it was in that of the Anglo-Saxons who also "conquered" New Mexico.

There were also wars within wars, the Spanish against Indians and Indians against Indians.

Raiders struck New Mexico from four directions. On the south was a Western Apache gauntlet through which supply caravans had to fight their way and which frequently disrupted communications between Mexico City and Santa Fe. Navajo raiders swept into the valley of the Rio Grande from the west with the regularity of the rising moon, and the colonial government was obliged to use most of its military force in counteroffensives against them. But the successes of these punitive expeditions were not lasting. From the east came Lipans, Faraons, and other Plains Apache raiders, ravaging farms, missions, and settlements, and making off with horses, mules, burros, sheep, cattle, and goats. So swiftly did they appear and vanish that pursuit would have been an exercise in futility, even if there had been soldiers available to undertake it, which seldom was the case. It was necessary to maintain a line of defense on the north for the purpose of repelling Utes and Comanches—or at least making it more difficult for them—but they broke through it, terrorizing colonists and pueblos and getting away with valuable booty.

The Ute also raided the Navajo in northwestern New

Mexico. Many of the Plains Apache in northwestern Texas, Oklahoma, western Kansas, and far northeastern New Mexico were in precarious positions, being imperiled by far-ranging Tonkawa, Tawakoni, Wichita, Pawnee, Kansa, and others from the southern Great Plains. The Plains Apache groups in El Cuartelejo were in desperate straits, continuing to plead with the Spanish for assistance against the Comanche, but receiving none. As early as 1705 the Comanche had moved through southeastern Colorado and were in northeastern New Mexico and the Texas Panhandle, steadily extending their deadly tentacles each ensuing year farther to the south.

Except for maintaining a few patrols along the northern frontier, in the Taos area, the Spanish, for reasons that cannot be explained, would not take serious cognizance of the growing Comanche menace until 1719. Their attention was fixed on the Faraon Plains Apache, who were making savage raids into southern and eastern New Mexico, as well as on the Rio Grande, and were regarded as a plague against which summary blows had to be taken at all costs. Thus, as Hyde states, the Spanish authorities ignored the operations of the Comanches, "and made no effort to assist the friendly Apache of eastern Colorado, who formed a protective screen for the New Mexican settlements and should have been assisted in their struggle to hold their lands."[2]

The first campaign of record against the Faraon had been made in 1702 by Governor Cuervó who destroyed several of their rancherias. In 1704, Governor Vargas, holding tenure as chief executive of the province a second time, died while pursuing a band of Faraon raiders in the Sandia Mountains. Two more small punitive expeditions had been sent against them in 1712 and 1714, but with minimal success, and their depredations had continued.

In 1715 the Faraon, accompanied by some Limita, Chipayne, and Tremintina, made a strong raid on Pecuris and

Taos pueblos in which they carried off several women and children, one of them a Spanish boy. Word reached Governor Juan Ignacio Flores Mogollón that large herds of stolen horses and mules were in the possession of these bands, and he decided to make an attempt to rescue the captives and teach these Plains Apache raiders a lesson they would not soon forget.

In a council of war held in Santa Fe late in July, both the Taos and the Picuris declared their willingness to assist the Spanish military and aid in the recruiting of men from other pueblos. Don Geronimo, governor of Taos, advised Mogollón that the best time to strike the Faraon rancherias "in order to take them together and to punish them is in the middle of August when the moon is almost full. At this time they are shaking out the grain from the ears of corn. Having finished doing this and having buried it beneath the soil, they all go on a hunt for buffalo where they maintain themselves until they return to sow which is at the end of April or the beginning of May. There they remain until they cut it. Soldiers will not find them in any other manner. . . ."

Don Lorenzo, chief of the Picuris, brought back from El Cuartelejo in 1706 by Ulibarri, informed Mogollón that "from Picuris pueblo to the first Faraon rancheria, composed of thirty houses of wood entirely smeared with clay outside, which is located on the banks of a river, there are ten days of marching with sufficient water every day [for a large number of cavalry] because the springs are large." The best trail, he declared, was by way of the Mora River. This latter detail was the only part of the advice given by Geronimo and Lorenzo that was adopted by Mogollón.

Not until August 26, more than a month after the Santa Fe council of war, did Governor Mogollón issue the orders necessary to set the campaign in motion. As commander he selected Captain Juan Páez Hurtado, instructing him to assemble his force at Picuris Pueblo and start from there August 30. No attack was to be made on any Plains Apache except the Faraon, whom Mogollón chose to identify as "Chipaines or Limitas." He warned Hurtado that other heathens encountered "shall not be maltreated in any respect," and to take care that Faraon women and children "are not killed and are apprehended and brought to my presence." These instructions may reflect to some degree the prevailing Spanish policy of attempting to win converts by displays of kindness, but it is more likely that they were issued to prevent colonists and the Pueblos with Hurtado, who had suffered in raids, from killing any Plains Apache in cold blood that they met along the line of march.

The Hurtado Expedition was the largest to be sent until this time from northern New Mexico against hostile Plains Apache. The roster illustrates the extent to which numerous Pueblo tribes had aligned themselves with the Spanish to fight raiders from the High Plains. As it made its way over the mountains east of Picuris toward the Mora River Valley the column was composed of one hundred and fifty-two Indian warriors from the pueblos of Picuris (eleven), San Ildefonso (sixteen), Santa Clara (twelve), San Juan (seventeen), Tesuque (eleven), Nambe (ten), Pujuaque (six), Taos (thirty-seven), and Pecos (thirty-two), all of them with two or more horses and half of them armed with guns.

The Spanish complement consisted of thirty-six professional soldiers of the ranks; fifty-two civilians of various callings, many of whom were members of the colonial militia; and one of whom was the notorious French traitor and murderer, Juan de L'Archeveque, now a militia captain; the noted scout and interpreter, Captain José Naranjo; and a chaplain, Fray Lucas Arebalo. Supplies were carried by a long packtrain of horses and mules, and the soldiers and colonists had among them nearly three hundred reserve mounts. In the Mora Valley the expedition would be joined by thirty Jicarilla and one warrior of the El Cuartelejo band, giving Hurtado a fighting force of two hundred and seventy-two men. Thus there is evidence that in order to hold the favor of the Spanish the Jicarilla were willing to fight other Plains Apache.

On September 4, camp was made on the Canadian River, and for the next nine or ten days, acting on the advice of Indian guides, Hurtado continued eastward into the valley of this stream. He wrote a daily report as he proceeded. Although it reveals his frustration, it amounts to little more than a description of the rugged country and an account of the inclemency of the weather.[3]

In traveling about two hundred miles east of Santa Fe, the expedition saw not a single Faraon. Several rancherias were found, but they were deserted and showed no sign of recent habitation. Tracks made by horses of Faraon bands were followed, but these trails split and ran away in all directions, each branch inevitably becoming less promising and at last vanishing into the sky.

On September 13 an Indian guide whom Hurtado does not identify informed him that a Faraon rancheria would be found about twenty miles ahead. He wrote in his report under this date, "I set out with forty-four soldiers and settlers and one hundred Indians to investigate a white sand hill which was near the spot and on which the guide said was the rancheria. Having marched some eight leagues, we came to an arroyo with much water and fine meadows of green pastures, but without a mark of having ever been a rancheria."

Infuriated, Hurtado demanded an explanation from the guide. Where were the houses and cornfields? But the guide spread his hands in a gesture of hopelessness and admitted "that he did not know where they were, that he was already confused and that he did not know where he was nor where he ought to go. Seeing that he was guilty of such negligence, I condemned him to be given fifty lashes with a whip. For this reason I called the place the Arroyo of the Whipping."

The next day a spring was reached where there were "old tracks of many people and horseherds who had gone out for buffalo."[4] Hurtado gave up and started back to Santa Fe.

In his report he made it appear that quite of his own accord he had come to the conclusion that in their trading at Pecos Pueblo the Faraon had learned that Mogollón was preparing to campaign against them. "For this reason," he wrote, "all the Faraon absented themselves from the Rio Colorado [Canadian River] where they have their rancherias."

He was right, but the deduction was not the fruit of his own cleverness. The seed for it had been planted two months earlier. At the July council called in Santa Fe for the purpose of discussing retaliatory measures to be taken against the Faraon, Don Geronimo had warned both Mogollón and Hurtado that in such an undertaking the people of Pecos were not to be trusted. The Faraon and the Pecos maintained close commercial ties, said the Taos leader, and as each derived great benefits from them neither would overlook an opportunity to help the other. The council record quoted Geronimo as saying emphatically that in case an expedition was to be sent against the Faraon "no Indians from Pecos should go because they will inform this nation [the Faraon] for the two are almost the same."

Scorning this advice, Mogollón had sent the *alcalde mayor* [Indian governor] of Pecos Pueblo a request for warriors to serve with the expedition under Hurtado, and the *alcalde mayor* had sent thirty-two. He also had sent couriers to the Faraon.

On September 30, 1715, Hurtado rode into Santa Fe, his campaign a complete failure.

4

Fray Juan de la Cruz was stationed in Taos, but his territorial jurisdiction included northeastern New Mexico and El Cuartelejo. He had little opportunity to minister to the Plains Apache of this vast region, not only because of the logistical problems involved but because the vicious, relentless attacks by the Comanche consistently dashed any hopes he had of conducting profitable missions among them.

For some time he had been profoundly saddened by the appeals of these Plains Apache groups for protection, supplications to which the provincial government appeared to be deaf. As a servant of God, he could not bring himself to advocate martial action against the Comanche, yet he understood very well that only through such aggressions could their destruction be halted and peace achieved.

At last he resorted to a plan that he was convinced was justified under the darkening aspect of the situation. Indeed, he felt assured that he was not in any sense neglecting his sacred duty, for he was doing no more than seeking the means of bringing more heathens into the fold. And that was work to which he had dedicated his life.

In the letter he dispatched early in 1719 to the Marquis de Valero, Viceroy of Mexico, no mention was made of the civil, political, or military problems confronting the Santa Fe government, and he praised Governor Valverde as a nobleman of much fear of God and religious zeal who "not only allays whatever troubles that may be encountered, but likewise encourages and aids us." This may have been diplomatically astute, but it was far from being the truth. Governor Antonio Valverde, who took office in 1717, was a man of many enemies, but contrary to the old adage this was not a reliable measure with which to judge either his qualifications or his character. He was corrupt, cold-blooded, cowardly, and hypocritical. He falsified his accounts, stole government stores, levied heavy taxes, which he pocketed, and cheated soldiers by charging them outrageous prices for the food and other necessities they required for their families.

"For some time," Father Cruz wrote Viceroy Valero, "I have found myself in the quiet and peaceful possession of my mission, the sole and only end of my journey from our beloved Spain to these countries. This consideration, Sir, for which I have voluntarily exiled myself, for the greater glory of God, does not excuse my concern and obligation to the person of your Excellency from writing these words.

"Considering then the holy desire of your Excellency to improve souls, especially in these parts where heathenism is so widely spread, I must look to your Excellency without doubt, whatever the undertaking will be, to bring with greater joy the light of the faith and disperse the shades of idolatry. I am, Sir, so close to heathenism, that, as is commonly said, we are shoulder to shoulder.

"A tribe of heathen Apache, a nation widely scattered in these parts, of whom it may be said [is] a matter of great good for the future, have come to ask for holy baptism. Having examined their intents and persuasions, I found them to be truly religious.

"In this affair I am now engaged, so that, it having been decided what ought to be done in a case of this kind, the immediate undertaking will continue."[1]

An opportunity to save Indian souls was seldom overlooked by a viceroy, but it was not only Fray Cruz's letter that brought Valero to a decision with somewhat unusual rapidity in the summer of 1719. Reports that the French were planning to invade both Texas and New Mexico had reached him. Although the stories were not supported by irrefutable evidence, he nevertheless chose to look upon the French as a threat that might develop into a serious situation, and he did not propose to be caught off guard.

The instructions he issued were terse: "With reference to what Father Cruz writes of the Apache Indians, let Governor Valverde be ordered to employ with the greatest efficiency all his care to allure and entertain them extensively . . . it is necessary to hold this nation because of the hostilities which the French have launched. . . . As the Apache nation aided by ourselves could inflict considerable damage on the French and block their evil designs, Governor Valverde must assist with all the people he can and on such occasions which offer themselves. . . . Father Cruz will be advised that the governor himself concurs in subjugating and entertaining the Apache Indians. . . ."[2]

Valverde was displeased. A journey of several hundred miles to the northeast could not be completed before cold weather, and possibly snows, had come to the High Plains. He would have preferred to postpone the task until spring. Yet he feared that such a delay might invoke the wrath of Valero, and perhaps result in his recall.

In its size Hurtado's expedition had established a postcolonization record, but the force Valverde assembled was more than twice as large. According to his own report, it consisted of sixty soldiers from the Santa Fe *presidio*, forty-five volunteer colonists, four hundred and sixty-five Pueblos, and some two hundred Plains Apache—Jicarilla, El Cuartelejo, Chalchufine, Fleches de Palos, Penxaye, and Carlana warriors—who joined him after he had crossed the mountains east of Taos. Fray de la Cruz was not asked to go along, Valverde selecting Fray Juan del Pino, minister at Pecos Pueblo, to serve as chaplain. As usual, Naranjo was chief of scouts.

Besides nearly a thousand horses and mules and a large band of sheep, in the column were long packtrains carrying equipment and supplies, among them great quantities of *pinole*, chocolate, tobacco, and presents for friendly Plains Apache. In Valverde's personal baggage were several casks of wine, a small keg of fine brandy, some glasses, and rich melon preserves, ostensibly to be used in celebrating important saints' days. Hunters were assigned to the duty of procuring for his larder turkeys, grouse, quail, venison, and buffalo steaks. Each night he set up camp for himself and the other Spaniards some distance from that of the Indians, and insisted that his own horses be kept apart from the others.[3]

Valverde broke no new trails, following the familiar route to the upper Canadian, over the high summit to the Purgatoire, and on to the Arkansas, descending it probably as far as the present town of La Junta, Colorado. On numerous occasions his camp was surrounded by a veritable horde of Plains Apache, who poured out their fears and recounted their sufferings. The Comanche, ever increasing in strength, were carrying off Apache women and children, stealing their horses and crops, burning their homes, keeping them from going on hunts. Their desperate plight was made evident by the sight of destroyed villages. In one rancheria alone more than sixty of them had been slain. The frequency of these attacks was growing to such an extent that many of them no longer knew where to go to live, and some of them had already fled great distances to the south and west, and if they were not aided by the Spaniards at once all of them would be forced to abandon their homeland.

Valverde was generous not only with gifts but in his promises that the Comanche would feel the force of Spanish arms, repeatedly assuring them that he had come to their land to save them and to punish the Comanche, and he counseled them to embrace without reservation the holy faith of the God in heaven, for in trusting Him they would find comfort and relief. One Plains Apache band literally accepted his advice, and although their inherent practicality somewhat strained their credulity they made a sincere effort to free themselves of the burden. This passage appears in the Valverde diary:

"Having come into the governor's presence, they dismounted at a distance of some fifteen steps. Their chief carried as a standard a most holy cross, at the foot of which was an engraved parchment, whereon there was an image of Mary, our most holy lady, in adoration of the rosary.[4] The chief, bearing in his hand so sovereign a standard without any injury whatsoever, gave it to the governor and the reverend chaplain to kiss, who did this with all veneration, and to the soldiers and settlers who had gathered at the news. After this incident had passed, touching as it was, because they all adored on their knees this most holy wooden symbol of our redemption, the governor welcomed the chief and all the rest."

After giving an account of their sufferings and losses at the hands of the Comanche, the Indians told Valverde, "Their greatest sorrow was that, since they had carefully wrapped up and guarded this image of the most holy Mary, they had found on opening it three drops of blood. For this reason they feared that something was going to happen to them. Upon hearing this with all attention and kindness, the governor told them they should not be disconsolate, and that they should keep the lady in their hearts, being certain that if they truly called upon her and reduced themselves to the fold of the church they might attain victory. The governor was setting out in person on a campaign to look for the Comanche enemy to make war upon them. The blood, he explained, which they said the most holy Lady had, signified that they should abandon their heathen and barbarous life in which they lived and make Christians of themselves. If they should decide upon doing this, she would aid and assist them in everything for their welfare and being. He set before them, with Catholic and Christian zeal, other effective arguments so that by this means their reduction could be achieved. The Apache chief with all the rest who accompanied him said that the governor was their father whom they loved a great deal since he spoke courteously to them, and was going to defend them. If the governor should wish it, said the chief, they would receive the water of holy baptism, upon which Valverde rejoiced greatly. The governor had chocolate given to them all and to the settlers who were there, and tobacco distributed among the heathens. He commanded that if they had need of anything, they should let it be known so that they could be helped immediately. They answered that they needed nothing [?]. After which the heathen went away quite satisfied, offering to accompany the governor on the campaign.''

No Comanche were found, although during October in El Cuartelejo several trails were discovered, but trackers pronounced them too old to be worth following. At one place they came upon a campsite of a very large band in which the ashes of more than two hundred cooking fires were counted. Usually in a force of this size an average of five persons used each fire, which meant that at least a thousand Comanche had paused to eat and rest. Naranjo estimated that the fires had been built no more than three or four days earlier.

The diary states that as the expedition proceeded "the track of the enemy was recognized, which left a clear trail wherever it went, both on account of the great number of

Comanche and their multitude of horses, as well as the tent poles they carried dragging along behind. Their road went northeast [that is, away from the Arkansas River]."

Valverde would state that he had been strongly in favor of pursuing the Comanche "until they should all be punished," but that he had been dissuaded from doing so by Captain Naranjo and Chief Carlana. These two counselors had advised him that the Comanche had taken a route along which there was very little water, not enough to support the horse herd and the command.

Valverde then advanced at a leisurely pace, doubtful that it would be wise to continue much farther, for it was late in October, the weather was turning cold and some snow already had fallen on the peaks to the west. He would maintain that he was greatly disappointed at not being able to overtake the Comanche, but that he was thoroughly "familiar with the snow and cold, which in these lands is so extreme that it benumbs and annihilates." He was also extremely regretful that he had been unable to learn anything about the activities of the French. However, his luck in this respect suddenly took a turn for the better.

A Paloma Plains Apache who was suffering from a gunshot wound that was not yet fully healed was brought to his tent. There, the report relates, "the governor examined the injury and asked him who had given it to him." Through Naranjo, who was fluent in the Apache language, the Paloma "answered that while he and his people were in their land,[5] the French united with the Pawnees and the Jumanos ambushed them while they were planting corn.[6] Placed on the defensive, they fought, and it was then that they gave him the oblique wound in the abdomen which was still healing. The Paloma also said that "had not night settled on them, so they could escape from their rancheria, none would have been alive. The Comanche seized the Paloma lands . . . and held them from that time on."

The statement of the wounded Paloma that the Jumano

Apache were in league with the French and Pawnee is baffling. The same charge had been made by Indians in Santa Fe on at least two previous occasions, but there is no documentary evidence to support it. In the eighteenth century the Jumano Apache were in southwestern Texas and southeastern New Mexico. There is no record to indicate that they ranged northward into western Kansas or that they were enemies of Plains Apache in that region. Nor is there historical material suggesting that up to this time El Cuartelejo Plains Apache had invaded Jumano territory. On linguistic and historical grounds, the Jumano are classified as Western Apache. While they periodically hunted buffalo along the Rio Pecos in Texas, they customarily returned to permanent settlements, some of them along the Rio Grande below New Mexico, in which they dwelt in houses constructed of rock and adobe. It is possible, however, that a small band of Jumano either were driven from their people or chose to separate from them, perhaps after a quarrel, became outlaws, and eventually found a haven among the Pawnee, but there is no proof.

The wounded Paloma's story got better as it progressed. The French, he allegedly declared, had built "two large pueblos, each of which is as large as that of Taos. In them they live together with the said Pawnees and Jumanos Indians, to whom they have given long guns which they taught them to shoot. They also carry small guns suspended from their belts." During the fight, the Paloma had shouted to the French that they would ask the Spanish for help, and "to this the French responded that they would be greatly pleased to have them notify the Spanish and bring them there, for the Spanish were women."

It was probably Naranjo who advised Valverde that the insult was customarily shouted by Indians at enemies in battle. Valverde stated that he was unperturbed, understanding that the rude words were used merely to incite ire. But he was not a little disturbed by the wounded Paloma's

assertion that besides the two towns comparable in size to
Taos, the French "have three other settlements on the other
side of the large river, and that from these they bring arms
and the rest of the things they bring to those [the great
pueblos] they have recently constructed. The Apache know
this because they were told by some women of their own
tribe who were made captives among the French, but who
had fled and returned." What Valverde obviously did not
understand was that the large river of which the Paloma was
speaking was the Missouri. Nor did he learn, although the
Plains Apache must have been apprised of the fact, that in
order to establish trade with the main bands of the Pawnee
and other tribes of the central Great Plains the French were
ascending the Platte River in Nebraska.

With little geographical knowledge to guide him, Valverde would write the Viceroy of his conclusion that the
posts of the French were about two hundred leagues from
Santa Fe. If he was unable to give them locations, he was
not far wrong in his estimate of the distance. He added that
he believed "the purposes of the French appear accordingly
to be to penetrate little by little inland. This country is very
suitable for doing this because of its abundant meat, game,
streams, and plains."

It was inconceivable to him that the French *voyageurs*
were more interested in trade and slaves than in conquering
New Mexico. To him they were a menace creeping like
dark storm clouds upon Spanish territory.

One distinguished scholar has remarked with due sarcasm
that Valverde's only achievement on his journey was to give
the name of a saint to every river, creek, and water hole
along his route. He accomplished something else that
deserves mention: By repeatedly swearing to the Plains
Apache that he would protect them from their enemies, he
perpetrated a vicious hoax and won for himself undying
notoriety as an unconscionable perjurer.

5

Unconfirmed reports often traveled with greater speed than official dispatches between Santa Fe and Mexico City. The source of the rumors that threw Viceroy Valero into a state of consternation as the year 1719 ended are unknown. However, if it cannot be entirely proved that Plains Apache leaders in El Cuartelejo had something to do with the dissemination of those rumors, the possibility must not be disregarded, for they were astute and clever men. Moreover, they were rapidly coming to realize that if they were to receive Spanish aid it would not be because they became converts to Christianity and were baptized but because of the Spanish government's fear of French encroachment.

In any case, Valverde's report of his expedition went forward "by His Majesty's mail" from Santa Fe to Valero on November 30. Eleven days later, Governor Manuel San Juan de Santa Cruz of the northern Mexican State of Nueva Vizcaya wrote the Viceroy in alarm that news had "come unexpectedly from a soldier passing through from New Mexico sent to your Excellency by its governor. The information, as the captains of Conchos, Campana, and the alcalde mayor of San Bartolemé gave it to me, is that seventy leagues from the villa of Santa Fe there are six thousand French. . . . They are drawing nearer, chiefly across open land, without forces or trained men able to resist them. Accordingly, they will come closer swiftly and easily."

Early in 1720, urgent orders went north to Valverde. He was to establish a *presidio* and a mission at a suitable location in El Cuartelejo, stationing there twenty-five soldiers and three priests. This to repel an army of six thousand French! The same order was sent to the Marqués de San Miguel, Spanish commander in Texas, to build a post of similar size among friendly Indians in the northern part of his jurisdiction. In addition, Valverde was to encourage the El Cuartelejo Apache, while the priests were converting them, to increase their cultivation of the land, to live in permanent settlements like the Pueblos and other sedentary tribes, and thus contribute to the creation of a buffer zone against French intrusion. Also, Valverde was to make a thorough reconnaissance to the northeast in the hope that new intelligence regarding the French might be obtained.

Valverde's conduct and practices may have been deserving of unqualified reprobation, but he could not be justifiably accused of either ignorance or density. If France had managed to send six thousand soldiers marching across the Great Plains, Spanish dominion north of Mexico was doomed. Even if such a miracle had not taken place, establishing a *presidio* and mission of any size in El Cuartelejo was totally impractical.

In restrained and diplomatic language Valverde communicated some of his thoughts on the matter to Viceroy Valero. Perhaps the haste that the contingency demanded was responsible for the error in judgment. The only suitable location in El Cuartelejo for a *presidio* was approximately three hundred and fifty miles from Santa Fe. Soldiers and missionaries sent there could not be properly protected

and supported. In his estimation, it would be more advantageous to establish the outpost among the Jicarilla Apache
northeast of Taos a short distance and only one hundred
miles from the seat of the New Mexican government. Not
only would the Jicarilla welcome it, but they would gladly
settle around it and aid, if necessary, in its defense.

Meanwhile, he informed Valero, he was preparing to lead
another expedition to search for the French, and he
expressed the hope that the Viceroy would amend his orders
in accordance with the suggestions he had made.

Valero and his advisers would accept Valverde's advice,
but before authority to change the location of the new *presidio* had reached him the reconnaissance had been completed. And with tragic results.

The actions of Valverde in the summer of 1720 would
never be explained to the satisfaction of the Viceroy and his
executives. Charges of negligence leveled against him would
result in his being severely censured and fined.

Instead of personally conducting an investigation to
determine the whereabouts and intentions of the French in
the northeast, as he had been ordered and had said he
would do, he had assigned Captain Pedro de Villasur to the
mission. It would be his contention that at the time he had
not been in good health, and, moreover, other urgent matters and obligations had made mandatory his continued
presence in Santa Fe. Investigative authorities, however,
would show that these excuses were without foundation.

Villasur himself would reveal to colleagues his own mys-
tification as to why the Governor had favored him with the
appointment. He was a young officer recently transferred
from an administrative post in Nueva Vizcaya to Santa Fe,
had taken part only briefly in campaigning against Indians,
and knew nothing at all about the country to which he was
being sent.

Valverde made another puzzling decision. He permitted

Villasur to take with him only forty-two soldiers, sixty Pueblos, three civilian colonists, and one priest, hardly a
sufficient force in view of the hazardous nature of the assign-
ment. Captain Naranjo and Juan de L'Archeveque, as
usual, went along as aides. The chaplain was Fray Juan
Minguez.

The company was well equipped and provisioned, the
supplies being carried on pack mules, and each member
being furnished with several reserve horses. Unencumbered
by sheep or cattle, it was in a position to travel fast. Several
accounts mention that sacks of maize, some short swords,
knives, sombreros, and a quantity of tobacco were taken as
gifts for Plains Apache who might be employed as guides.
One soldier would state that Villasur had for his own use
several silver dishes, a saltcellar, an inkhorn, quill pens,
writing paper, silver spoons, and a candlestick.

There is no complete detailed report of the Villasur
reconnaissance. Copies of a portion of a diary, evidently
written by an aide, covering only five or six days, have been
preserved in several libraries.[1]

Villasur led his command northward out of Santa Fe
about July 1. At Picuris, or perhaps Taos, they crossed the
mountains, following the customary trail to the northeast.
Plains Apache, probably Jicarilla and Carlana, willingly
guided them to the Arkansas in El Cuartelejo. Thus far no
Comanche or Pawnee had been encountered, but when Villasur announced his intention to continue northward,
directly into the country of their enemies, the friendly
Plains Apache only shook their heads, as if in despair, and
bade him farewell.

All that is certain about the route followed from the
Arkansas is that it ran toward the northeast. Traveling
across vast plains on which immense herds of game grazed
—probably for more than a fortnight—in August they came
to a stream which they called Rio Jesús Maria. It was the

south fork of the Platte. They had gone farther north than any previous Spanish military expedition—west central Nebraska—but although they were on a main east-west trade trail between the Missouri River and the Rocky Mountains, in one of the richest hunting grounds of the Great Plains, no Indians or fresh trails left by them had been found.

Villasur summoned his officers and aides to a council. An important decision had to be made. The brief diary states: "We decided to camp in order to see what had to be done. Villasur set forth for consideration the length of the journey we had made, which in his belief was about three hundred leagues [nearly eight hundred miles]. Then he proposed for consideration whether we ought to try to discover . . . if there were any French established in these regions, or whether, since we had not up to the present found any . . . we should continue our search among the Pawnee nation, the only one which may be able to give us some light, through which we might be able to communicate with the French.

"All were of the opinion that it was necessary to look for the Pawnees to learn the truth from them, or to learn whether the Apache had deceived us."

For the next four days they descended the South Platte. They were nearing its junction with the North Platte when a member of a scouting party that had gone ahead returned to report "that eight leagues from us, on the other side of the stream which we were following, they had found the Pawnees in a bottom, singing and dancing according to the custom of savages. There had appeared to be a large number of them. It was not judged fit to approach them nearer for fear of frightening them in the night." The company forded the South Platte, advanced for three leagues, and made camp.

One of the colonists, Christophe de la Serne, had with

him a Pawnee servant who had been taken from his people as a boy—presumably by Indians—and sold in the Taos slave market. As he could still speak his native tongue, it was decided to send him ahead to assure the Pawnee that the Spaniards came in peace, their only objective to learn if any French were in the country.

The first attempt of the envoy failed. When he was seen approaching the Pawnee village, although he gave the customary signs of friendship, "many savages came toward him . . . four who walked ahead of the band with hatchets in their hands, uttering cries." He became frightened and fled on his horse back to the Spaniards.

Villasur led his command along the north bank of the Platte, a short distance below the junction, and halted opposite the campgrounds of the Pawnee. A crowd of Indians stood at the edge of the water, shouting and gesturing. The Pawnee emissary informed Villasur that they were making signs of peace and were calling for one person to talk with them.

This is the essential part of the last entry in the diary remnant:

"The savage of Serne decided to cross to the other side, notwithstanding the fear he had had the day before. . . . Villasur instructed him to tell his nation that he was coming to see them and without any intention of causing them the least injury. . . . He gave some tobacco to the savage to take to them, which is the reasoning ordinarily used in these conversations. . . ."

The Pawnee swam across the stream and disappeared. Shortly he reappeared on the bank and shouted that he had been taken prisoner and would not be allowed to return. The Spaniards never saw him again.

Not a little angered by the cold rejection of his friendly efforts, Villasur urged in a council that the company charge across the river and force the Pawnee to provide him with the information he desired regarding the French. Naranjo, L'Archeveque, and other experienced frontiersmen dissuaded him from making the attempt, interpreting the actions of the Pawnee as a warning. As it was late in the afternoon, they advised that a retreat be made up the river to some place safer than their present exposed location.

The troop moved upstream, passing the point where the rivers divided, crossed the North Platte, and made camp on the slender tongue of land separating the two streams. The horses were turned out to graze, mounted sentries were posted, a meal was cooked, and the men soon retired. During the night a Pueblo guard reported that a dog was barking nearby and that he had heard some splashing in the river to the south, but a squad sent to investigate returned, having seen no one in the area.

It was August 14, 1720.

At dawn several hundred Pawnee warriors attacked with such suddenness that Villasur and a number of others were slain before they could fire their guns. The Pueblos panicked and escaped with many of the horses, but not before eleven of them had died. The Spanish soldiers fought with great bravery, taking a heavy toll of Pawnee, but only twelve of them, almost all badly wounded, would be among the living when, after no more than thirty minutes of fighting, the attackers suddenly retreated across the South Platte. Among the forty-two dead, lying near Villasur, were Captain Naranjo, L'Archeveque, Fray Minguez, and two colonists.

Some of the Pawnee casualties were armed with French guns and wore French jackets and caps.

Nearly a month passed before the survivors straggled into Santa Fe. All of the expedition's supplies and equipment had been lost, but necessities had been furnished to them by Plains Apache, who had been awaiting the company's return south of the Arkansas in El Cuartelejo.

Valverde sent special couriers racing to Mexico City with the sad news. Besides losing a third of his best soldiers, he was burdened with the responsibility of caring for thirty-two widows and many orphans. Expressing the fear that an invasion by French and Pawnee might be imminent, and warning that his stores and equipment were at dangerously low levels, he pleaded for reinforcements. Moreover, he declared, in his weakened condition he was without the means to launch forceful offensives against the Navajo, Ute, Comanche, and Faraon Apache, all of whom were striking at every opportunity against the colony's settlements and pueblos, while engaged in deadly combat with each other.

Alarmed by Villasur's defeat and the generally bad conditions in New Mexico, the Viceroy proposed, among other things, that a strong *presidio* be established in El Cuartelejo, but execution of the plan was delayed by red tape and conflicting opinions about a *presidio's* practicality. The story that a powerful French army was moving toward Santa Fe had turned out to be a myth. International relations had improved. The Franco-Spanish war that had begun in 1719 had lasted only until August 1720, and under the terms of the peace France had returned to Spain posts captured in western Florida and Texas. All danger of a French military conquest on the Rio Grande had been removed. It was realized that French traders would continue their activities on the Mississippi, the Missouri, and the Great Plains—they already had reached the Rocky Mountains—but they were not looked upon as posing a serious threat to Spanish territory. Some officials felt that the intertribal warfare that was raging north and northeast of New Mexico in itself would force the curtailment of foreign commerce. Without doubt the French were trading with the Pawnee, but the possibility of their establishing amicable relationships with the Apache of the High Plains, in view of the traditional enmity between the two peoples, was exceedingly remote.

The bones of Villasur and those who had died with him had lain, white and picked clean by animals, beside the Rio Jesús Maria for six years before exhaustive studies, inquiries, and field investigations produced a decisive policy regarding the problems of New Mexico. In 1726, officials in Spain and Mexico finally reached an accord which maintained the following:

The task to be faced in the colony was its protection from Indian raiders. This could be best accomplished by substantially increasing both provincial defenses and the number of priests to convert more heathens. Efforts to extend the empire northeast of New Mexico would involve a useless and heavy drain on the national treasury. If the Plains Apache, or any other wild tribe, required and wanted aid against enemies, let them move into the Rio Grande Valley or areas close to it, where there were vast sections of unoccupied cultivatable lands, and where they would be under the protection of Spanish guns, Spanish laws, and the cross of Christianity.

There would never be a Spanish *presidio* or mission in El Cuartelejo.

The Spanish decisions, so confidently contrived, would bring no relief to the harassed colony of New Mexico, and to the Plains Apache they would serve only to speed the advance of disaster. At the beginning of the eighteenth century the Plains Apache had held undisputed control of the High Plains from western Texas to the Black Hills of South Dakota. In the following years they had attempted throughout this vast region to develop a higher culture than it was possible for a nomadic people to enjoy who subsisted by hunting and gathering wild plant foods. They had turned to agriculture; they were anxious to engage in animal husbandry; and they had attempted to establish permanent villages. At the same time they had looked forward to continuing to procure the natural game and vegetable bounties of their country in sufficient quantities to meet their own needs and to maintain the old intertribal commerce from which they were benefiting long before Coronado's chronicler, Castañeda, wrote that some of them went west each year to trade at the pueblos and others journeyed far on similar missions in the direction of the Arkansas River and toward the Gulf of Mexico.

Not only other tribes and French *voyageurs* were responsible for the destruction of this emerging civilization. Spanish provincial laws forbade free trade in firearms with all Indians, and violators suffered severe punishment. Even those whose friendship had been demonstrated could not be legally provided for with any real assistance, as Hyde states, "until after they had given up their freedom and accepted the life of submissive slavery at Spanish missions. . . . The Jicarillas, El Cuartelejos, and Palomas gave abundant evidence of their wish to be on good terms with the Spaniards from 1700 to 1720. These Apache and Padoucas had more horses than any of the tribes that were attacking them, and all they needed to hold their lands and to form a barrier of friendly tribes along the New Mexican border was a more liberal Spanish trade policy that would permit them to obtain proper weapons and particularly firearms. Speaking blandly at councils and giving voice to earnest wishes to aid these Indian allies, the Spanish officials only tightened the trade restrictions and sat and watched the disaster sweep the screen of friendly Apache from their northeastern borders, to be quickly replaced by hostile Comanches, equipped by free French traders with better guns than any Spanish soldier in New Mexico was permitted to carry."[2]

Religious bigotry was the cause of this blindness. Spanish war and Indian policies having to do with wild tribes on New Mexico's northeastern frontier were based on theological principles. However, it is important to note that the prescribed formula did not completely prevent perversions.

Indeed, some of the courses of action that were officially sanctioned and pursued reached into the realm of incredibility.

In the case of the friendly Plains Apache, for example, the premise of the decision to refuse them aid was that they could save themselves by abandoning their homelands and their possessions and running from their enemies into Christianity's fold through the gates that had been opened to them. It was contended that by contributing matériel and thereby enabling them to defend themselves the Spanish monarch would be condoning their savagery. Moreover, the argument was advanced that after their unqualified acceptance of the faith and baptism they wouldn't need guns.

Yet, in regard to the Comanche problem the Spanish adopted a drastically different procedure. No one expected them to accept baptism or cease their barbarous practices. However, full endorsement was given to the idea that if they were allowed to attend trade fairs without danger from the Spanish military they would be brought into close contact with Christian influences. These fairs were held annually, and more often in some years, at Taos, Picuris, Pecos, and other places, and authorities gave support to the hypothesis that if the privilege of participating freely in them was denied to the Comanche their chances of finding salvation—admittedly very small—would be decreased.

This relaxation of strained relations was quite acceptable to the Comanches, not because they were in the least interested in rubbing elbows with missionaries or hearing church bells but because they were eager to barter slaves taken in their raids for Spanish goods and products produced by Pueblos. Besides cloth, metal articles, and all types of gewgaws, they coveted the bright little tin crosses offered by Spanish traders, which by some curious course of reasoning they looked upon as decorations especially appropriate when worn in warfare.

PART SIX

Chronicle of Disaster

1

Between 1700 and 1720 the trade in Padouca Apache captives steadily increased. The buyers were French traders operating in Kansas and Nebraska and on the lower Arkansas, the Missouri, and the Mississippi Rivers. The Skidi Pawnee, at the time the largest and militarily the strongest nation of the region, were the principal sellers. However, the Oto, Kansa, Iowa, and some other tribes also engaged in this traffic in human flesh. All of them were imbued with an intense and indestructible hatred for the Plains Apache, from whose incursions they had suffered for centuries before the weapons of white men at last gave them the means of gaining the revenge they had always craved.

Thus the heavy losses now being sustained by the Padoucas were directly attributable to an economic imbalance which pinioned many of them in untenable positions. Spanish and Pueblo products reached them through trade with other Plains Apache groups dwelling closer to New Mexico, but, like their kinsmen in El Cuartelejo, the commodities they needed most—guns, powder, and lead—were excluded from this commerce by Spanish trade laws. They were not totally without firearms, for they captured some in warfare, and some of British manufacture were obtained from upper Missouri River tribes with whom they maintained friendly relations and who were willing to exchange them for badly needed horses and the bright blue-green pieces of turquoise so greatly prized by all people of the northern Great Plains. However, those they had managed to acquire were far too few in number to provide them with the defensive, much less the offensive, power they required. Moreover, these weapons were unusable most of the time, for little ammunition came into their hands, and the small quantities they were able to get, either by trade or capture, were quickly consumed. This was not so serious a handicap for their antagonists, for a relatively dependable flow of French supplies reached them from the lower Missouri and the Mississippi Valleys.

The range of the Padoucas had been enormous after they had acquired horses, extending from western Nebraska, almost to the Missouri River, and southward through Kansas and Oklahoma to Texas, but after 1700 growing pressure from enemies, especially that of the Pawnees, had forced them to restrict their roving. Most of them concentrated in permanent villages—some of which were very large—although these settlements were widely scattered. They engaged in agriculture, as did most Plains Apache of the period, but invaders frequently destroyed crops in the field and stole stores from them.

The attacks by the well-armed Pawnee and other raiders were disastrous to the Padoucas, and by 1720 these Indians were well on the road to becoming hopelessly demoralized, if not quite yet a completely shattered people. The French paid the highest prices for young men, young women, and children, and the raiders directed their efforts toward taking these prizes. Not infrequently as many as two hundred, and on some occasions three hundred, were captured in a single raid.

In prehistoric warfare, or even in conflicts taking place in early historical times, the death of half a dozen warriors in a single engagement was looked upon as a heavy loss. But this was not traditional Indian warfare. It was an entirely new kind of combat in which hatchets and bows and arrows were pitted against the insuperable power of guns. And actually not many guns were needed. A dozen would quickly turn the tide of battle in favor of the invaders, terrorizing the Padoucas, sending them into desperate flight and bringing certain death to those who made courageous stands with their primitive weapons. In clashes that lasted no more than an hour or two whole villages were laid waste, hundreds of defenders were left dead in the ruins, and hundreds more were marched away as salable captives.

But not all the captured Padoucas lived long enough to be sold into slavery. Many of the women and children were cooked and eaten.

"Mainly interested in profits," writes Hyde, "the French traders were outraged over the Caddoan custom of eating women and children captives." Citing several occasions on which these grisly feasts are a matter of record, he adds, "One company of French traders had their business ruined because of this custom of the Black Pawnees, whose villages were on the Arkansas in eastern Oklahoma. The traders made the long journey to the villages in the summer of 1720 to trade for slaves and horses; but on their arrival they found that these Pawnees, who had recently destroyed a Padouca village, had already killed nearly all of the one hundred Padouca women and children captives. There is no record of Oklahoma Indians torturing captives by burning at the stake. There is plenty of evidence of cannibalism."[1]

Villasur's expedition to western Kansas and central

Nebraska, even though it had ended in disaster, alarmed officials in Paris, leading them to suspect that the Spanish were planning to draw into their own sphere of influence Indians of the Arkansas and Platte regions. This encompassment, if accomplished, would open new competitive commercial channels, obviously harmful to the Louisiana Territory Indian trade, a trade that was not only becoming more lucrative each year but also proffered possibilities for unlimited development. The larger part of the vast realm between the Missouri River and the Rocky Mountains was still almost totally unexplored, but Indians who lived in it, or claimed to have wandered through it, had been encountered, and, if what they told about its natural assets could be believed, it appeared to be incredibly rich in furs.

The French government did what the Spanish government had no intention of doing. That was to endeavor to lengthen its arteries of trade both directly westward to the mountains and southwestward to tribes known to be trading with the Spanish in New Mexico—the Apache of the High Plains.

The plan presented many problems, but one was seen as demanding the most urgent attention. It involved cementing an accord with the Padoucas.

Only the French, unhampered by ecclesiastical decrees that had the force of civil laws, with their superb talent for wilderness diplomacy and their extraordinary ability to maintain harmonious relationships with wild Indians, could have accomplished such a feat. If the emissaries assigned to the mission had gone directly to the Padoucas, they would have failed to achieve their objective; they would have been branded as turncoats by all the Padoucas' enemies, and the trade monopoly they held among those tribes would have been lost, perhaps beyond any possibility of recovery. They went first to the Pawnee, the Kansa, the Oto, and the Iowa. The councils that took place were long and exhausting.

Progress came with aggravating slowness, but the patience of the French, the shrewdness of their arguments, and their generous gifts at last brought them victory.

In the fall of 1724, chiefs of the Padouca, Kansa, Pawnee, Oto, and Iowa agreed to the peace proposed by the French. The trade in Padouca captives was halted. French guns were presented to the Padouca delegates by men who a few weeks earlier had been their deadliest foes. The Pawnee, Kansa, Oto, and Iowa would receive in return badly needed horses, which the Padouca possessed in large numbers. Now the way had been opened for French traders to extend their operations close to the Spanish borders through lands occupied by allies, and they soon pushed on to El Cuartelejo in far western Kansas.

E. V. de Bourgmond, a veteran Missouri River trader and the leader of the French negotiators, reported that the Padouca chief with whom he dealt had several thousand persons under his control. This tribe, he declared, roamed over an immense area reaching westward to the mountains and from the South Loup River (Nebraska) to the Cimarron River (New Mexico). In one village he visited there were eight hundred warriors, fifteen hundred women, and two thousand children. His people, said the chief, occupied eleven other villages.

Bourgmond retired and returned to France. The peace between the Padouca, Kansa, Pawnee, Oto, and Iowa probably lasted no more than two years. It was not the former enemies of the Padouca but the French themselves who destroyed it.

The French traders on the Missouri and Mississippi had never approved the plan initiated by the Paris officials, accusing them of being ignorant of the conditions prevailing on the Great Plains. The truth was that the peace had halted the highly profitable trade in Padouca captives and horses, and they had learned that the Plains Apache were not industrious producers of furs or other marketable goods. These men, upon whom the colony of Louisiana depended for the greater part of its revenues, launched a concerted effort to have the pact with the Padoucas officially revoked, and in 1728 they succeeded, the colonial council complying with their demands.

A paucity of details occurs in the historical record at this point. Indeed, it appears that raids against the Padoucas had been resumed a year or more earlier, perhaps in 1726, by the Pawnee and others, with sanction from the French. At the same time, French traders had established contacts with the Comanche, had sold them some guns and ammunition, and had reported them to be far more enterprising than the Padouca or other groups of Plains Apache. Acting with their customary perfidiousness, the French traders abandoned the Plains Apache, anticipating new and more profitable relationships with the Comanche. Some historians hold the view that the Padoucas were a destroyed people as early as 1727. Certainly by 1730 they had been driven out of Kansas and a large part of Nebraska. There is evidence to indicate that many of them fled into eastern New Mexico and the Panhandle of Texas, but how many is not known. There they would have been in the path of the Comanche onslaughts.

The Kansas and southern Nebraska Padoucas were gone from their old homelands, as if swept away and scattered by some supernatural wind. Nothing more was ever heard of them.

The Padoucas of northwestern Nebraska fared somewhat better. They had strong friends among the Kiowas of the Black Hills, and they traded with the Mandans and Arikaras on the upper Missouri. Moreover, in their remote location they were far north of the advancing Comanches, who, after emerging from the mountains in southern Colorado, pushed southward into Texas. As late as 1770 it was known to

French *voyageurs* that some Padouca were still living immediately south of the Black Hills. But by this time a new and
powerful enemy, the Dakota Sioux, was pushing westward
from the Missouri, steadily gaining control of the plains and
badlands of western South Dakota and western Nebraska in
vicious aggressions. By the end of the eighteenth century,
perhaps no later than 1785, the Padoucas of these regions
also had vanished. Where they went remains a mystery.

2

When French traders returned to El Cuartelejo in 1727 they met no Plains Apache.

The nine groups that had lived there were gone. These were the Paloma, Conejero, El Cuartelejo, Chalchufine, Carlana, Fleches de Palos, Penxaye, Rio Colorados, and Achos.

The Comanches were in control of the entire region and pushing their bloody conquest steadily southward into Oklahoma, Texas, and New Mexico. The French may have joined them in attacks on fugitive Plains Apache bands in New Mexico. In any case they negotiated an alliance with the Comanches, supplied them with guns and ammunition, and promised to return the following summer with more weapons to trade, a prospect very pleasing to the Comanche, who fully understood that no firearms could be obtained from the Spanish.

It seems possible that four of the Plains Apache bands of El Cuartelejo—the Conejero, Achos, Fleches de Palos, and Rio Colorado—may have been wiped out, for their names do not appear again in any record. However, a few families or individuals may have joined other groups and have lost their identity. It is believed that the survivors of the Penx-aye fled to the Jicarilla, to whom they were related. The El Cuartelejo debacle may be likened to a jigsaw puzzle from which some essential pieces are missing. Thus, blank spaces must forever remain in the historical picture.

In 1726 the daring and unrelenting Comanche drove a mixed group of Paloma and Chalchufine to the outskirts of Santa Fe. There the trail of these particular refugees is lost. However, it is known that some Plains Apache found homes among the Navajo west of the Jemez Range, and perhaps they were among those who in this manner disappeared from recorded history. But the possibility that they, too, found refuge among the Jicarilla may not be excluded.

Every El Cuartelejo group had been broken up; even families had been scattered, with little or no chance of ever being reunited. The new groups that emerged were composed of people of various bands who had joined together in desperate attempts to save themselves. Dramatically illustrating this confused situation were some Paloma, Carlana, and remnants of the El Cuartelejo band who moved southward to Pecos Pueblo, to which since far back in prehistoric times so many Plains Apache had gone to trade. There they waged a valiant struggle to support themselves by building small rancherias on streams near Pecos and by hunting. Hyde states that these people "went off into the plains eastward to support themselves by hunting buffalo, coming back to their rancherias in spring to plant and in late summer to harvest their crops. In alliance with the Pecos Indians, they had that ancient pueblo town to fall back on in case of enemy assaults on them. In need of horses—they had probably lost a great many during the Comanche raids on them—these Apache made friends with the Faraons and obtained new supplies of horses from them."[1]

The attacks would come, for the Comanche were not satisfied with having driven the Plains Apache out of El Cuartelejo, and Comanche war parties were roaming the Llano Estacado, never ceasing their attempts to kill more Plains Apache men and to capture Plains Apache women and children to be traded to the French for weapons. The buffalo hunts were perilous exploits, to be undertaken only with the greatest caution, and frequently they had to be abandoned because the hunters came upon trails of Comanche slave hunters.

The Plains Apache who settled near Pecos received no aid from the Spanish. On the contrary, they fell into Spanish disfavor because of their association with the Faraons. This group was continuing to make fierce and deadly raids on Spanish ranchos, settlements, and missions, as well as on Rio Grande Valley pueblos. Almost all the horses they possessed carried Spanish brands. When it became known that the Plains Apache near Pecos were friendly with the Faraons, officials in Santa Fe charged that they were aiding and abetting the Faraons, or even participating in the Faraon raids. The accusations were false.

Despite the precariousness of their situation and the doubtfulness of their security, the Plains Apache near Pecos managed to maintain a relatively meager existence for almost a decade. Perhaps the Comanche had not been certain of their whereabouts, or perhaps they had been occupied with raiding in the Taos district and in Oklahoma and Texas. Whatever may have been the reason for the delay of the Comanche attacks, they came at last with cyclonic ferocity. The year is not certain, but there can be no mistake that the devastation that had been carried out in El Cuartelejo was repeated. If on a smaller scale in this instance, it was no less vicious, no less complete.

Apparently Pecos Pueblo was not a major objective of the Comanche. It was attacked, but not in a sustained offensive, and it suffered little damage. But the refugees of the broken Paloma, Carlana, and El Cuartelejo bands came close to being annihilated. Their little rancherias, their stores of food, all their possessions, including most of their horses, were destroyed or taken away.

Now the Pecos made clear their unwillingness to provide the survivors with protection, giving two reasons for withdrawing their hospitality. They feared that if they permitted these helpless Plains Apache to live in the pueblo or even close to it, their presence would bring more attacks by the Comanche. Also, the Pecos were not unaware that the Spanish now regarded the Faraons as the worst heretics and villains of all wild Indians of New Mexico, and that the Plains Apache from El Cuartelejo had been condemned by the Spanish for their friendship with the Faraons. Thus, if they were allowed to remain, the Spanish governor might charge them with giving haven to miscreants and inflict penalties on them.

Once more these Plains Apache, destitute and homeless, were forced to move on. Where they went is not known, for they were never heard of again.[2]

3

Spanish treasure hunters traversing the high, flat country east and northeast of New Mexico after 1600 encountered the Faraon and other bands closely affiliated with them— such as their kinsmen, the Limita, Chipayne, and Tremintina—but recorded no tribal designations, speaking of them simply as people, and sometimes as Apaches, of the buffalo plains. Not until 1675 did the term *Faraon* appear in Spanish documents, at which time a campaign against "the Apaches called Pharaones and other natives joined with them" was being planned.[1] There is no adequate explanation as to why this peculiar name—which sometimes was spelled *Pharaohs*—was applied to a wild Plains Apache group. Some Spaniards may have thought that either in character or custom they resembled Egyptians, but this is conjecture.

When De Vargas left El Paso in 1693 and moved northward along the Rio Grande with hundreds of colonists and soldiers to complete his reconquest of New Mexico, the ever-watchful Faraons, Limitas, Chipaynes, and Tremintinas sent word ahead to both the Pueblos and other Apache

that he was returning. Before De Vargas had reached Santa
Fe most of the main Pueblo tribes and all but one of the
Apache groups—the Faraons and their allied relatives—had
pledged themselves to fight the invaders. The Pecos adopted
a policy of attempting to make peace with the Spaniards.
Commercial ties influenced the decision of the Faraon amalgamation. These bands were good friends of the Pecos and
had for many years enjoyed a profitable trade with them.
They, therefore, feared that by siding with the others they
would antagonize their best customers, and they elected to
make every effort to stay out of the coming conflict.

The most northern range of the Faraon at this time was
the watershed of the Canadian River in extreme northeastern New Mexico.[2] On this stream, its south fork, and smaller
affluents they had for at least three decades, if not longer,
maintained small rancherias on which the principal crop
grown was maize. However, some of their farms were farther
east in Oklahoma and Texas. It was their custom, as it was
with other Plains Apache peoples, to leave these permanent
homes after spring planting and to spend the summer
months hunting. They still subsisted mainly on buffalo,
other game, and wild vegetal foods, and pemmican and
hides were the chief commodities they brought into Pecos
and other pueblos to trade.

Not only were they strong enough to guard their own territory, which extended far down the Pecos to the vicinity of
the present New Mexico town of Roswell, against invaders,
but they were feared raiders. They sent war parties eastward
against the Texas Caddoan tribes and westward against
pueblos in the Manzano Mountains and the Rio Grande
Valley.

Not long after the Spanish had recovered New Mexico
and had subdued most of the Pueblos, the structure of the
Faraon economy began to undergo drastic changes.

As previously noted, it had been their hope that by avoid-

ing a direct confrontation with the returning Spanish the
Faraon would be able to preserve their profitable commercial relations with Pecos and other towns. However, they
had not been altogether scrupulous in adhering to this
policy. The temptations to raid, especially for those living
between the Rio Pecos and the Canadian River, had been
too great to be resisted. Bands struck against caravans and
ranchos from time to time with no little success, and they
swiftly had achieved the stature of a serious menace. When
soldiers could be spared from other fronts, punitive expeditions had been sent out against them, but on almost every
occasion the Indians had managed to slip away without
suffering serious losses.

Several factors caused the Faraon to make a complete
about-face after twelve or thirteen years of doing no more
than spasmodically bedeviling the colony. They could no
longer follow their traditional life customs and could no
longer conduct their trading under conditions advantageous
to them. That time had gone, its end brought about by
Comanche inroads on the eastern New Mexico and western
Texas plains, by the increasing military strength of the
Spanish, and by the growing number of armed civilians and
Pueblo Indians available for campaigns against them. By
1715 the Faraons had become full-fledged relentless raiders,
striking against both Spanish settlements and pueblos with
wild fury. They swept into the Rio Grande Valley in powerful parties, burning buildings, killing settlers, and driving
away large herds of horses, mules, and donkeys. Spanish
counteroffensives had little effect on their deadly incursions.

The Comanche succeeded where the Spanish failed.

Before 1720 the Comanche hordes had destroyed the
Faraon rancherias on the Canadian River, and had driven
them southward to the Rio Pecos.

Continuing their attacks, a few years later, the Comanche

had forced the Faraon to scatter and to abandon the High Plains along the entire length of the New Mexico-Texas border. Flight eastward was not possible, for along the upper Red River they would have come up against their ancient enemies, the Caddoans, who were now liberally armed, as were the Comanche, with French firearms.

Unlike many other Plains Apache bands, the retreat of the Faraon, Limita, Chipayne, and Tremintina can be delineated with a certain degree of accuracy. Fleeing south-westward from the Rio Pecos, they reappeared after the passage of some years under a new tribal name: Mescaleros.

The territory over which they now roved lay on both sides of the Rio Grande in south central New Mexico. On the west it extended almost to the headwaters of the Gila River, and on the east to the Sierra Blanca, Pajarito, and Sacramento mountain ranges. This large, rough, arid area afforded them considerable protection, and from it, often joining other Apache, these Indians rode on raids up and down the Rio Grande Valley, eastward into Texas, and deep into Mexico.

The designations *Limita, Chipayne,* and *Tremintina* vanished from history, but the name *Faraon* has been preserved to this day. Although they lived for centuries among the Apache of the High Plains, the Faraon are now classified by scholars as a division of the Mescalero group, and on linguistic grounds placed among the Western Apache.

4

The Lipan and Teya, as stated at the beginning of this work, were the first Plains Apache to be encountered by Europeans. Núñez Cabeza de Vaca met the Teya on the plateau of western Texas in 1535, and six years later Coronado's men found them and the Lipan in northeastern New Mexico and the Texas Panhandle. Perhaps these Spanish pathfinders also met the Natagee and Lipiyane, who were consanguineously close to the Lipan, but that will never be ascertained, for the names *Natagee* and *Lipiyane* do not appear soon enough in Spanish chronicles to suggest such a possibility.

The names *Teya, Natagee,* and *Lipiyane* disappeared from New Mexican reports at early dates. However, discontinuance of their use did not mean that colonials believed these Plains Apache had ceased to exist—not at all. It meant simply that Santa Fe officials were no longer able to account for them as distinct groups, for the reason that they had lost their respective identities either in alliances or through a mysterious process of absorption by other larger tribes.

Although the names by which the Spanish first knew them are, and always will be, perpetuated in history, what happened to them after they were driven from the Llano Estacado of eastern New Mexico and northwestern Texas can never be known in detail, and, actually, for the most part must remain in the realm of speculation. The Teya were the first to vanish under the identity Castañeda gave to them. As they were a branch of the Lipan, the most logical assumption seems to be that they were completely absorbed by that tribe, the largest of all Plains Apache groups.

But the same thing cannot be said of the Natagee and Lipiyane, for they continued to be mentioned in records long after the Teya's fate had been sealed. They moved to southern New Mexico, for some time dwelling west of the Rio Grande, and ultimately disappeared in that conglomeration of Plains Apache remnants to be known as the Mescaleros.

Many of the Piro and Tewa pueblos east of the Rio Grande and along the river had been destroyed by Lipans from the plains of eastern New Mexico and western Texas before the time of the Coronado Expedition. These raiders were the Lipan Teyas. Coronado called the Lipans he met east of the Rio Pecos in New Mexico and in the Texas Panhandle *Querechos*. Fifty years later this name was still heard, but soon after the colonization of New Mexico it was supplanted by *Llanero*. When Zaldivar, Oñate's nephew, took a company to the Canadian River in 1598, the Llanero Lipan asked him for aid in fighting the Jumano. The Jumano were Western Apache. Núñez Cabeza de Vaca had discovered them in 1535, at which time they were living along the Rio Grande below El Paso. He learned that they journeyed regularly to hunt buffalo on the plains along the Pecos in Texas, and for that reason he called them the Nation of the Cows. Espejo reported meeting some of them in the same area forty-eight years later, but it seems apparent that by this time they were beginning to range farther north and east of the Rio Pecos in New Mexico, for when Zaldivar explored the Canadian, war parties of Jumano were attacking the Lipan in the region of that river.

Looking farther toward the northeast, we find the Escanjaques appealing to Oñate in the year 1601, on the plains of Kansas, to join them in attacking the Caddoans, who dwelt to the east on the Arkansas River, and who were raiding them, taking a heavy toll in lives and stealing their property. Oñate not only refused to help them but he prevented them from destroying Caddoan villages he visited. The Escanjaques of Oñate were Lipans, called *Cantsi* by the Texas Caddoans.

Thus, it becomes clear that at least as early as the final decade of the seventeenth century the branches of the Lipans who since far back in prehistoric times had held supreme control of the High Plains of eastern New Mexico, northern Texas, and parts of southern Kansas were suffering from strong enemy pressures on three fronts. The Jumano Apache, disdainful of kinship, were raiding them from the south. The Caddoan tribes of Kansas and Texas were attacking them from the east and northeast. If they had not as yet inflicted any serious damage on them, the Spanish, concentrating in the upper Rio Grande Valley, stood as a potential danger in the country of the Pueblos to the west.

Probably the Escanjaques, who came close to destroying the Oñate Expedition in an all-day battle, were the first of the northern Lipans to leave their traditional homeland. This exodus evidently took place during the first quarter of the seventeenth century. It is believed that they resettled on the upper Red River in Texas, a territory in which there were numerous groups of Lipan. After Oñate's tenure in New Mexico they became a "lost tribe," their name never again heard.

But if in the early years of the seventeeth century the military prowess of the Lipans was not superior to that of their antagonists from the southern Great Plains, that was not true by 1650. Even before this time they had begun to acquire horses, both by trading and raiding, from tribes in southern New Mexico, northern Mexico, and in western Texas below El Paso, and perhaps gaining a few that had strayed or that they had managed to steal from Spanish caravans. The number of mounts they obtained increased each year, giving them incomparable powers as warriors, which they applied with deadly effect against their old enemies, the Caddoans.

"These Apache mounted raids in the seventeenth century," writes Hyde, "brought about profound changes in the southern plains. The primitive times of slow movements of small camps of foot Indians, of friendly relations with other tribes, made more interesting by occasional raids, were ended; and into the plains came stark war, the destruction of entire villages at a blow, and slavery on a commercial scale. . . . Caddoan tribes abandoned many of their open and undefended villages to draw together in large groups on the Arkansas River in eastern Oklahoma, where many fragments of population from their older settlements were crowded together for mutual defense."[1]

With the turn of the century came a decisive turn in the fortunes of the Caddoans. They had not only begun to acquire some horses, the sources of which are uncertain, but, more important, they were obtaining firearms from French traders. The tide of warfare rose steadily against the Lipan bastions, and they found themselves unable to stand against it. Like so many of their kinsmen in El Cuartelejo, they sought in vain to obtain guns from the Spanish. Their only alternative was to defend themselves as best they could against the inexorable power of Caddoan guns with the poor weapons they possessed, bows and arrows and some

Spanish axes, knives, and saber blades, while they withdrew with the hope of reaching territory into which their attackers might hesitate to venture.

The retreat of the Lipan was not a rout. They were in serious danger of being disastrously defeated in 1720, but saved themselves by keeping out of the way of the Caddoans and by cautious shiftings. In 1730 they still occupied much of the Red River country and had settlements in the upper valleys of the Colorado and Brazos Rivers. Despite their lack of guns—although by this time they had obtained some in warfare and forays against Spanish settlements in eastern Texas—they made fierce raids against Spanish missions and ranchos in the San Antonio district and other parts of south Texas.

By 1735 all Lipan were gone from the upper Red River district, and that area was being occupied by the Caddoan Tawehash, who were soon joined by the Caddoan Tawakonis. Both of these tribes had been forced to leave their Arkansas River towns by the Siouan Osage. The northern boundary of the Lipan range was now the upper Colorado River; however, the Lipans roamed far south of it, sometimes raiding westward into New Mexico and southward into Mexico, for nearly a decade remaining a formidable force that contributed greatly to inhibiting Spanish plans in Texas.

Then suddenly the Lipan raids all but halted. The Spanish in San Antonio, who had always slept with their guns beside them, could only wonder at the change, but they would soon come to understand the reasons for it.

Perhaps as early as 1740 the Comanche had begun to make friends and to trade with the Caddoans on the Red River. From these villages strong bands of Comanche and Caddoan warriors had pushed southward, and within a short time had launched full-scale attacks on the Lipans.

Spanish officials were amazed when, in 1750, Lipan emis-

saries appeared in San Antonio and, avowing that hence-
forth they would be obedient and friendly, asked that a mission be built for them so that they could learn to become
good Christians.

If the Spaniards were delighted by this unexpected turn
of affairs, they were not so gullible as to be unable to realize
that the Lipans were desperately seeking their protection.
All hope of converting any Apache had long before been
abandoned. Still they believed that miracles happened, and
the Lipans' request was duly dispatched to Mexico City.

It took officials six years to decide the matter. Meanwhile,
the Lipans were widely scattered, presumably constantly
harassed by the Comanche and Caddoans, and probably suffering grievously from their combined onslaughts. At last,
in 1756 the mission was approved. The site selected for it
was on the Rio San Saba, a tributary of the Rio Colorado, in
the present Menard County of Texas. As usual, a small military contingent was assigned to protect it. It was opened for
services in the spring of 1757.

A large number of Lipan were soon camped nearby, but
suddenly all but three or four who were incapacitated vanished. Those who remained were housed within its walls. A
few days later a horde of Comanches and Caddoans, heavily
armed with French guns, attacked. Within a few hours the
San Saba mission had been reduced to ashes, its occupants
slaughtered.

The Lipans had never intended to subject themselves to
the religious discipline of the Catholic Church. They had
believed, or at least hoped, that a mission with a complement of soldiers and armed civilians might serve to deter
Comanche aggressions along the Rio Colorado. The swift
sacking of the San Saba mission had shown them that the
Comanche had no intention of curtailing their southward
advance. They withdrew again, most of them into the
rugged plateau and mountain country of southwestern

Texas, but others went on into Mexico, and some crossed the Rio Pecos, merging with refugee bands from other groups, perhaps joining the Mescaleros west of the Rio Grande.[2]

Seeing themselves in danger of losing Texas to the wild tribes from the north, the Spanish assembled five hundred soldiers and several artillery pieces for the purpose of mounting a campaign against them. Now, in a strange about-face, they asked the Lipan for help, and the Lipan gave it. Out of their southwestern Texas retreats came a large band of Lipan warriors. From the vicinity of San Antonio they guided the Spanish force to enemy strongholds on the Red River. A Caddoan village was taken, several score of the defenders being slain, and the others driven into precipitous flight. Flushed with this victory, in which the Lipan exhibited extraordinary bravery, the column marched on up the river, searching for more enemy camps to conquer.

One was found. Not far from the present city of Wichita Falls they came upon a great fort. A moat surrounded it, and on the inner bank were tall wooden palisades. Inside this formidable sprawling structure were some six thousand Comanches and Caddoans.

The Spanish cannon opened fire, but the balls did little damage against the timbers, and in an attempt to cross the moat the soldiers were driven back by a withering fusillade, suffering a number of casualties. The Lipan had seen enough. They departed.

Convinced that further efforts to break through the defenses would be costly and futile, the Spanish, abandoning some of their cannon, set out in a rapid retreat. They narrowly escaped from disaster, for bands of Comanche, well equipped with French guns, maintained a running fight, and Spanish ammunition was extremely low when the soldiers, ragged and hungry, reached San Antonio.

Texas was in a desperate plight. If the colonists had been

given their own way they would have scurried for Mexico, but the missionaries, unflinching under the threat of martyrdom, were determined to remain, and Spanish officials acquiesced to the demand of the Church that new efforts be made to save the colony.

Blinded to the realities of the situation by their indestructible religious fanaticism, the priests obtained authority to establish two new missions. Called Candelaria and San Lorenzo, they were built in 1761-62 on the San Antonio River. About four hundred Lipans were induced to settle on adjoining farmlands, but each spring, after planting crops, they left on what they said were hunting trips but which more often turned out to be raids into Mexico. They construed mass and other church rituals as entertainment, to be enjoyed when they had nothing more practical to do, and they refused baptism. They also refused to cease adhering to their own ancient spiritual beliefs. They sang and danced to their own supernaturals, while the chapels stood empty.

By the priests' own admission, Candelaria and San Lorenzo were abysmal failures. In 1767 both church and government appropriations for them were halted, and they were left to fall into dust.

The Comanche, having extended their vicious raids to the Gulf of Mexico below San Antonio, turned westward, plunging beyond the Rio Grande into the richer provinces of northern Mexico.

The Lipan, striving to keep out of their way, were broken into relatively small bands. They made their homes mainly in the Big Bend country and the Davis Mountains. From this region they continued to strike at Spanish settlements both in southwestern Texas and across the border in the Mexican province of Coahuila, but by the end of the eighteenth century they were well along the earthly road to extinction.

The story of the Indian wars of the nineteenth century is

beyond the scope of this history, but perhaps a few details regarding the ultimate fate of the Lipans properly should be set down here. Most of the Texas Lipans, whom Newcomb states had become "the skulking, beggarly riffraff of the Texas frontier," had been driven by United States soldiers and Rangers into Mexico by 1850.[3] That this characterization cannot justifiably be applied to all of them is shown by an event that took place in 1853.

In that year, the Mexican state of Coahuila, which had long suffered heavily from Lipan raids emanating from the United States, devised a scheme by which it hoped to gain a large measure of relief from the menace. It sent delegates to negotiate an agreement with Wild Cat, leader of a strong band of Lipan still holding out in the Davis Mountains of Texas. Under its terms, if he and his people would migrate from the United States to Coahuila, each family would be given ten acres of farm land. In return for this generous gift, Coahuila expected them to pledge themselves to protect the state from all Indian raiders. Wild Cat accepted the offer and crossed the Rio Grande with some three hundred warriors and their women and children. Coahuila gained the relief it sought, but Texas paid the bill. Wild Cat interpreted the understanding as giving him unlimited license to conduct raids into the United States. Angrily, American officials complained that seldom a month passed in which Wild Cat and his warriors did not kill Texans, destroy property, and steal livestock and merchandise. After perpetrating these barbarities the Lipan recrossed the Rio Grande and found security from pursuit and punishment in Mexico. Coahuila made no attempt to convince Wild Cat that his comprehension of the pact was based on an erroneous assumption, but in time American military forces would succeed where the Coahuilans had been negligent.

In 1905 the American government, acting on a request

made by Mexico, agreed to transfer all Lipan still in Coahuila to the Mescalero Reservation in New Mexico. It wasn't an undertaking difficult to carry out, for only nineteen Lipan were still living.

5

The Jicarilla are the only Plains Apache who still occupy
lands in close proximity to the region in which they were
first discovered by white men, the Spanish treasure hunters
of the sixteenth century. They live in northwestern New
Mexico,[1] on a reservation relatively well endowed with natural resources but infinitesimal in size compared to the vast
domain through which they once roamed, the High Plains
washing against the southernmost barriers of the Rocky
Mountains.

How they were driven from their traditional homeland
by the Utes and Comanches, and how the Spanish refused to
supply them with the weapons that would have enabled
them to defend themselves, are subjects treated in preceding
pages. By 1750 they had become a broken tribe, perhaps
saved from complete annihilation only by the compact they
had long maintained with the people of Taos and Picuris,
pueblos in which many of them found sanctuary in times of
great danger from invaders.[2] In the succeeding forty or fifty
years, the Jicarilla, steadfastly and contemptuously defying
all efforts of priests to convert them to Christianity—a mis-

sion built for them was soon abandoned—endured a precarious existence. The buffalo plains along the Canadian River in eastern New Mexico and in El Cuartelejo, where they had for centuries obtained the products that made it possible for them to engage in profitable commerce with other tribes, had been closed to them since 1730. They had little to trade, almost nothing but a few pelts obtained in the mountains immediately surrounding them in the Taos area and some little baskets and pottery vessels which their women manufactured. Suffering this poverty, never without fear of being attacked, they managed to subsist on small crops of maize and beans, wild fruits and nuts and roots, and by venturing cautiously from their little hidden villages in search of small game, seldom more than a step ahead of hunger.

Then they changed. It was as if, by some strange psychological phenomenon, a new spirit had been aroused in them, transposing apathy and defeatism into vigorous action and bold defiance of the forces that had long held them in suppression.

They became outlaws, plunderers, vicious killers, lurking like wolves in mountain recesses and emerging to strike with deadly fury on their chosen prey.

The launching of the revolution to free themselves from Spain by the Mexicans in 1810 opened a decade of unprecedented political and economic turmoil in New Mexico, turmoil that not only played into the hands of the Western Apache but all belligerent Indians in the north of the colony: the Navajo, the Jicarilla, and renegade Pueblos. They subjected the Rio Grande Valley and its environs to a reign of terror, and no military reinforcements came from Mexico; indeed, the beleaguered Spanish colonial government withdrew troops from the northern frontier to fight the rebellious Mexicans. Spanish officials in Santa Fe, with only small garrisons available to them and supplies rapidly

dwindling, were in desperate straits; they were in no position to wage campaigns sufficiently effective to curtail, much
less halt, Indian depredations. Moreover, augmenting the
pressure on them was the growing dissension among the colonists, many of whom obviously cared little whether Spain
or Mexico was victorious. They were thinking of their own
skins, unswayed by loyalties or patriotic emotions.

It is improbable, however, that either the officials or the
ignorant settlers of the upper Rio Grande region realized in
their fears that one factor alone provided them with a large
measure of security. That was the inability, or the unwillingness, of the Indians to organize. If no more than five
thousand Indians had overcome, even temporarily, the prej-
udices and hatreds that normally dominated them, merged
their forces, and attacked in cooperation with each other,
New Mexico would have known the same fate it suffered as
a result of the uprising of 1680. It would have become once
again a vast theater of intertribal wars, with the Comanche
sweeping in from the High Plains, the Utes from the north,
the Navajo from the west, the Apaches from the south to
battle for the prize, with the Pueblos fighting among themselves, in the middle. As it was, the small professional military contingents left on the upper Rio Grande, with the aid
of Indian mercenaries and fragments of the once strong
civilian militia, were frequently successful in inflicting
severe punishment on raiders. If these strikes had little decisive effect and the fighting was halted for only brief periods,
they, nevertheless, saved New Mexico.

The Jicarilla were never in their history one of the largest
Plains Apache tribes, but they made up for their lack of
numbers on the warpath in the first decades of the nineteenth century with clever and merciless brigandage. The
change of flags over New Mexico—1821 from Spanish to
Mexican, in 1846 from Mexican to American—had no effect
whatsoever on their barbarous operations. And two things

should not be forgotten: (a) long before the American conquest, in their raids they had acquired all the horses, guns,
and ammunition they needed to continue their depredations with telling success; (b) a band of no more than two
hundred warriors, mounted, heavily armed, highly mobile,
and intimately familiar with the country, comprised a most
dangerous force.

The first American Indian agent assigned to New Mexico
reached Santa Fe in the summer of 1849. He was James S.
Calhoun, a close friend of President Zachary Taylor. In the
Mexican War he had served with distinction and had risen
to the rank of lieutenant colonel. Although he had no previous experience in Indian affairs, he would soon demon-
strate that he was qualified to handle the problems confronting him. His reports were unusually blunt, objective, critical, and devoid of political mumbo jumbo. He would make
mistakes, but his sincerity and personal integrity were above
question.

Calhoun learned quickly that all troubles involving the
Apache were by no means in southern New Mexico. The
northern part of the territory had its share. However, not all
of them could be blamed directly on the Jicarilla. Not a few
were the result of wanton acts committed by American
troopers, traders, and ranchers. One tragic occurrence
attracted national attention. An assistant Indian agent
reported to Calhoun in October 1849 that near Las Vegas,
east of Santa Fe, a group of soldiers had fired without cause
or provocation into a small band of Jicarilla, killing and
wounding several of them.

The Jicarilla had not waited long to take revenge.
According to an Indian office report, E. J. White with his
wife and infant daughter and several other persons were
traveling with a wagon train to Santa Fe, where White for-
merly had engaged in trade. When the caravan had passed
through the part of the country considered dangerous, west

of Las Vegas, the Whites set out ahead of the slow vehicles, accompanied by a German named Lawberger, an unidentified American, a Mexican, and a Negro servant. A band of Jicarilla attacked them, killing all the men, and taking the woman and child captive.

A troop of soldiers was soon in pursuit of the raiders. They were tracked down and several of them were slain, but it was learned that Mrs. White had been murdered already and the little girl had been carried away to an unknown destination.

The federal government offered to pay a thousand dollars to the Jicarilla, either in money or merchandise of equal value, if they would return the child, but without success. She was never found.

The official account adds a statement made by James A. Bennett, a trooper who participated in the search for the Jicarilla slayers: "One evening a noise was heard near our camp. At first we supposed it to be an animal of some kind. Three or four of us made an examination through the willow bushes and found an Indian child which I suppose was about eight months old. It was strapped to a board as all Indian babies are. I found it. An old gruff soldier stepped up and said, 'Let me see that brat.' I handed it to him. He picked up a heavy stone, tied it to the board, dashed baby and all into the stream, and in a moment no trace of it was left. The soldier's only comment was, 'You're a little fellow now but will make a big Injun bye and bye. I only wish I had more to treat the same way.' "

The Jicarilla, now aided by some Utes and a few survivors of other Plains Apache bands that had been destroyed, kept up their attacks on travelers and small wagon trains on the trails to Santa Fe and Taos. In one fight in 1850 eleven white men escorting United States mail met death. Patrols were constantly in search of the raiders, overtaking some, but these operations failed to produce any lasting results. The attacks continued spasmodically, making necessary the sending of strong forces of guards with caravans.

After months of diplomatic effort, Calhoun was able to persuade Jicarilla leaders to meet with him under a flag of truce. Several councils were held, and at last he convinced them that they were fighting a losing war and eventually would be wiped out. A treaty of peace was signed. Under its terms, the Jicarilla were to be awarded lands on which they could develop farms and graze livestock. The government would supply them with agricultural instruments and instructors, pay them a monthly annuity, and furnish them with rations and clothing until they were able to sustain themselves. It was a noteworthy accomplishment, and Calhoun deserved the gratitude of the people of New Mexico and the approbation of the highest officers of the government. Instead he was criticized and his feat was ignored. The people of New Mexico, especially the American population, wanted the Jicarilla imprisoned in a concentration camp or, preferably, executed as bandits. In Washington the treaty was ensconced in some Senate pigeonhole and forgotten. It would never be ratified by that body, as required by law.

In 1851, Calhoun was appointed governor of New Mexico, but he continued to serve as superintendent of Indian affairs. He and his aides found themselves in the unenviable position of having to inform the Jicarilla—more than two hundred and fifty Jicarilla families already had moved to their new treaty home—that the promises made to them would not be fulfilled by the Great White Father.

In their disillusionment, and once more facing poverty, the Jicarilla saw no alternative but to return to the warpath. Within a few months their depredations had become so extensive that a large military force had to be kept in the field in a campaign against them. They would suffer a severe defeat by United States troops in 1854, and were forced to live on the immense Maxwell grant area in northeastern New Mexico, where necessities barely sufficient to keep them from starving or freezing to death were doled out to them. There they were imprisoned for sixteen years.

Washington seemed unable to resolve the problem of what to do with them, but a decision was forced by the sale of the Maxwell grant, necessitating their removal. They became helpless pawns enmeshed in bureaucratic red tape. In 1872 and 1873 some officials recommended that they be taken to Fort Stanton [in Lincoln County, New Mexico], but this proposal was overruled, and most of them were permitted to go to the vicinity of the Tierra Amarilla [Rio Arriba County], almost on the Colorado border in northwestern New Mexico. In 1878, when they refused to move south to a remote arid area, their annuities were discontinued. Hungry and destitute, they raided ranches in a desperate struggle to keep themselves alive.

The wrangling in Washington continued. In 1880 the annuities were restored to them, on the theory that it was more economical to give them something to eat and to wear than to protect their victims with troops. A new reservation was set aside for them on the Navajo River, and they willingly went to it. But three years later they were rounded up like cattle and sent to Fort Stanton, where they were held until 1887. In this year an executive order established the reservation they still occupy, and where eventually they were allotted land in severalty.

Of all the many groups that once comprised the great Plains Apache branch of the Athapascan family, only the Jicarilla survived long enough to enjoy permanent security in the world of white mankind. Indeed, in some respects they enjoy what may be termed a modestly prosperous economy. They own commercial timberlands and grazing lands in considerable quantities. Large parts of their reservation are high and scenic, affording tourist attractions. Oil and gas have been found and developed, providing a steady flow of funds into the tribal coffers. There are no buffalo, but each family is entitled to own one hundred and fifty head of beef cattle. The Jicarilla council recently invested a large sum in a Hollywood motion picture production, and made a profit.

Notes

PART ONE

Chapter One

1 Modern place names are used throughout this work to make it easier for readers to locate the scenes of events.

2 They would make the first crossing of the continent north of central Mexico.

Chapter Two

1 Origin myths of the Athapascan Navajo relate that some of their people emerged into life beside the western sea. The Apache have no such tradition.

Chapter Three

1 The Kiowa-Apache are considered in a separate chapter. John R. Swanton, in his *Indian Tribes of North America,* says they also called themselves *Nadisha-dena,* meaning "our people."

PART TWO

Chapter Two

[1] In his *The Indians of Texas*. See also Opler (1945); Dennis and Dennis (1925), and Terrell (1972). Full citations for these and other books mentioned in the footnotes are in the Bibliography.

[2] Skins, weapons, ornaments, and, in later times, horses and firearms.

[3] *Land of Poco Tiempo.* . . . .

[4] In Plains Apache mythology the direction of all movements is from north to south, obviously reflecting upon their early migration southward from the far north.

Chapter Three

[1] *The Narrative of the Expedition of Coronado,* translated by George Parker Winship (q.v.).

[2] This statement should be qualified with the notation that Coronado had engaged guides, natives of the Quivira region, who had been captives of the Pecos Pueblos, and who were expert in the sign language, a highly efficient gesture system used by each tribe of the Great Plains to communicate with people whose tongues were different from their own. The Spaniards knew no Indian language, although they might have acquired in a short time some understanding of signs.

[3] The Spanish judicial league was equivalent to 2.63 English miles.

[4] Both the names *Querechos* and *Teyas* were used by some Pueblos to identify the Plains Apache. Castañeda probably first heard the names when the expedition passed through various pueblos, either on the Rio Grande or east of that river.

[5] First known mention of the apparatus to which French *voyageurs* would give the name *travois*. It consisted of two slender poles extending from a harness worn by dogs, dragging on the ground. Much larger *travois*, capable of holding heavy loads, were pulled at a later time by horses. Used throughout the Great Plains.

[6] Probably dark gray.

[7] A *sanbenito* was a piece of cloth, perhaps a yard in length, with an opening in the center. It was pulled over the head, resting on the shoulders, and hanging down both front and back. *Sanbenitos* worn in sixteenth-century Spanish churches had a Saint Andrews cross, usually made of red cloth, sewn onto each flap.

[8] Albinos were known to exist among western Indians, and the expedition probably had seen one.

PART THREE

Chapter One

1 Documents, letters, and accounts of the Coronado Expedition, including Castañeda's narrative, had been interred in the disorderly files of the government in Seville, not to be resurrected and translated into French and English until the nineteenth century.

Chapter Two

1 *The Rediscovery of New Mexico,* edited and translated by Hammond and Rey, contains a translation of the Gallegos papers.

2 As it is beyond the scope of this work, the entire journey of the Rodrigues-Chamuscado Expedition will not be recounted in detail. With a few exceptions, only the part pertaining to the Plains Apache will be included here. Similar treatment will be accorded later expeditions.

3 An *arroba* equals about twenty-five pounds.

4 An unidentifiable tributary of the Canadian River, in extreme eastern New Mexico.

5 Following Coronado's trail, they went on through extreme cold and deep snow as far west as Zuni, returning by the same route.

6 At the present Bernalillo, New Mexico.

7 Very rich ore.

Chapter Three

1 Four friars had intended to go, but only one would make the journey, the others being withdrawn to fulfill different church assignments.

2 Although it was translated and published earlier, a new translation appears in the 1966 edition of Hammond and Rey's *The Rediscovery of New Mexico.*

3 They would reach Mexico in safety, but an account of their homeward journey, if, indeed, one was written, has not been found in Spanish archives.

Chapter Four

1 Espejo had died in Havana in 1586, while en route to Spain. He had been informed that, despite his criminal record, he ranked high among contenders for the appointment, and it was his belief that he

would be victorious if he could plead his case personally before high officials in Seville.

[2] A translation appears in Hammond and Rey's *The Rediscovery of New Mexico*. These authors suggest that perhaps the *Memoria* was written by Castano's secretary, Andres Perez de Verlanga. It was first published by Pacheco y Cardenas in Spain.

[3] There were many salines in far western Texas and southeastern New Mexico before the Pecos was controlled by dams and the development or irrigation projects.

[4] Seventeen miles above Bernalillo, New Mexico, on the Rio Grande. It is still occupied.

Chapter Five

[1] On the Rio Grande about twenty miles northwest of Santa Fe. It is still occupied.

[2] Perhaps it should be remarked that there are innumerable recorded instances of Indians, in all parts of the United States region, fabricating the kinds of tales they shrewdly detected that white invaders wanted most to hear.

[3] Translations of Jusepe's statement appear in Bolton's *Spanish Explorations in the Southwest* and in Hammond and Rey's *The Rediscovery of New Mexico* and *Don Juan de Oñate: Colonizer of New Mexico, 1595-1638*.

PART FOUR

Chapter One

[1] Oñate left San Gabriel early in October, but as the exploration has no bearing upon the history of the Plains Apache, it will be omitted.

[2] Bolton's *Spanish Explorers in the Southwest* contains a translation of Zaldivar's report, a copy of which is preserved in the Archives of the Indies, Seville.

[3] Jack D. Forbes in *Apache, Navajo and Spaniard,* quoting from a manuscript by Juan de Villagutierre in the National Library of Madrid.

[4] Hammond and Rey made a translation of Zaldivar's report from a photograph copy of the document preserved in the Archives of the

Indies. It appears in their *Don Juan de Oñate, Colonizer of New Mexico, 1595–1638.*

⁵ The quotes on pp. 92–93 are from Hammond and Rey translation, *op. cit.*

Chapter Three

¹ The identity of the account's author is uncertain, but religious phraseology and repeated references to saints and holy days suggest that it was drafted for Oñate by Fray Velasco. Fray Vergara, the other friar with the company, could not write. Copies of the document are preserved in the Archives of the Indies and the Library of Congress. Translations have been published in several works, among them Bolton's *Spanish Explorers in the Southwest* and Hammond and Rey's *Don Juan de Oñate, Colonizer of New Mexico, 1595–1638.*

² A name that many Spaniards used in speaking of the buffalo, and that was also applied to the territory of the Pueblos.

³ The statements of the two soldiers, Martinez and Rodriguez, are published in translation in Hammond and Rey's *Don Juan de Oñate, Colonizer of New Mexico, 1595–1638.*

⁴ A Wichita word meaning "chief."

Chapter Four

¹ A translation of Benavides's memorial was made by Mrs. Edward E. Ayer, and privately printed in Chicago in 1916. It was annotated by Frederick Webb Hodge of the Bureau of American Ethnology and the distinguished historian and scholar, Charles Fletcher Lummis.

² This physical punishment was still inflicted in the nineteenth century by the Western Apache in southern New Mexico and Arizona.

PART FIVE

Chapter One

¹ *Indians of the High Plains.*

² The Spanish were first to use the name *Comanche* in written documents, but until recent years its origin and meaning remained a puzzle. In 1943 anthropologist Marvin K. Opler successfully traced it to the language of the Ute. It derived from the Ute word *Komantcia,*

which in the fullest sense means "anyone who wants to fight me all the time." The Spanish got it from the Ute, and to Spanish ears it sounded like *Comanche*.

[3] A. B. Thomas, *After Coronado*.

Chapter Two

[1] An English translation of the Ulibarri diary is published in Thomas's *After Coronado*. A copy of the original manuscript is owned by the Bancroft Library, University of California, Berkeley.

[2] Also Plains Apache.

[3] From the account one is led to believe that the Indians accompanying the Spaniards might have been confused as to exactly where the company wished to go. It is difficult to believe that the Indian guides would have wandered from a trail in a country in which they lived and hunted.

[4] A soldier would state later in Santa Fe that the "other spoils" included several guns, clothes, small short swords, French iron axes, and the foot of a gilded silver chalice. The soldier would swear under oath that he saw these articles.

Chapter Three

[1] In *After Coronado*.

[2] In *Indians of the High Plains*.

[3] A translation of the Hurtado report was made by Thomas and published in his work *After Coronado*. The original manuscript is owned by the Bancroft Library, University of California, Berkeley.

[4] They were now in the Texas Panhandle, perhaps not a great distance northwest of the present city of Amarillo.

Chapter Four

[1] Bancroft, *History of Arizona and New Mexico*; Forbes, *Apache, Navajo and Spaniards;* Terrell, *Apache Chronicle;* Thomas, *After Coronado*. Fray Cruz's letter is quoted from Thomas.

[2] From Thomas, *After Coronado*.

[3] A so-called diary of Valverde's journey was sent to the Viceroy, but its author is uncertain. Most probably it was kept by one of his aides or secretaries. Thomas, who made a translation of the account (in his *After Coronado*), notes that the last pages were destroyed. The manu-

script is in the Bancroft Library, University of California, Berkeley. See also Bancroft's *History of Arizona and New Mexico*; Twitchell's *The Spanish Archives of New Mexico*; Hyde*s Indians of the High Plains*; Terrell's *Apache Chronicle*.

4 Where the Indians had obtained these articles is not explained, but it seems apparent they had been lost by some previous expedition.

5 South of the Arkansas River, in western Kansas.

6 Perhaps the writer of the diary intended to say "harvesting corn," for planting was usually done in late May; unless the Paloma was suffering from a serious infection, the gunshot wound would have been healed before late October.

Chapter Five

1 Translations into English have been made by A. E. Sheldon, *Nebraska History Quarterly* (1923), and Thomas, *After Coronado*. See also A. F. A. Bandelier, *Contributions to the History of the Southwestern Portion of the United States*; Bancroft, *History of Arizona and New Mexico*; Twitchell, *Leading Facts of New Mexico History*.

2 Hyde, *Indians of the High Plains*.

PART SIX

Chapter One

1 Hyde, *Indians of the High Plains*.

Chapter Two

1 *Indians of the High Plains*.

2 It might be noted that in 1744, long after all the El Cuartelejo Plains Apache had gone from the area, the Comanche attacked Pecos in force. They struck this time not from the north but from the Llano Estacado to the east. A number of Pecos Indians were slain, but the Comanche were driven off. Two years later they came back and almost succeeded in sacking the pueblo. Although they killed a large number of defenders, they were not able to breach the strong walls, and after withdrawing they raided Spanish settlements and ranchos in the Galisteo Valley, only twenty miles from Santa Fe. Now it was they who were the scourge of northern New Mexico, and the Spanish, abandoning their religious policies, at long last launched a war against them.

Chapter Three

[1] Forbes, *Apache, Navajo and Spaniard.*

[2] Hereafter the Limita, Chipayne, and Tremintina will be included without specific reference to them under the name *Faraon.*

Chapter Four

[1] *Indians of the High Plains.*

[2] All the dispossessed Plains Apache who reached southern New Mexico eventually would be absorbed by Western Apache tribes in western New Mexico and Arizona.

[3] Newcomb, *The Indians of Texas.*

Chapter Five

[1] Rio Arriba and Sandoval counties.

[2] It was, by the way, an economic and military accord never violated by any of the three parties.

Selected Bibliography

ABEL, ANNIE HELOISE, *The Official Correspondence of James S. Calhoun While Indian Agent at Santa Fe and Superintendent of Indian Affairs in New Mexico,* Washington, 1915.

ALVARADO, HERNANDO DE, and JUAN DE PADILLA, *"Account of Journey from Cibola to the Rio Grande Pueblos in 1540."* Translation in Winship (q.v.).

BANCROFT, HUBERT HOWE, *History of Utah, 1540–1887,* San Francisco, 1891.

———, *History of Nevada, Colorado and Wyoming,* San Francisco, 1890.

———, *History of Mexico,* San Francisco, 1883.

———, *History of Arizona and New Mexico,* San Francisco, 1889.

———, *History of North Mexican States and Texas,* 2 vols., San Francisco, 1884.

———, *Native Races,* Vols. 1 to 5, San Francisco, 1886–1890.

BANDELIER, ADOLPH F. A., *Final Report of Investigations Among the Indians of the Southwestern United States,* 2 vols., Cambridge, 1890.

———, *Contributions to the History of the Southwestern Portion of the United States,* Cambridge, 1890.

———, and FANNY BANDELIER, *Historical Documents Relating to New Mexico*, Carnegie Institution, Washington, 1937.

BANDELIER, FANNY, *The Journey of Álvar Núñez Cabeza de Vaca and His Companions from Florida to the Pacific, 1528–1536.* Translated from the 1542 edition of Cabeza de Vaca's *Relación*. New York, 1905.

BECK, WARREN A., *New Mexico, a History of Four Centuries*, Norman, 1969.

BENAVIDES, FRAY ALONSO DE, *Memorial of 1630* (Mrs. Edward E. Ayer, translator), Chicago, 1916: Reprinted Albuquerque, 1965.

BENEDICT, RUTH, *Patterns of Culture*, New York, 1934.

BISHOP, MORRIS, *The Odyssey of Cabeza de Vaca*, New York, 1933.

BOAS, FRANZ, *Race, Language and Culture*, New York, 1949.

BOLTON, HERBERT EUGENE, *The Spanish Borderlands*, New Haven, 1921.

——— (editor), *Spanish Explorers in the Southwest*, New York, 1916.

———, "The Jumano Indians of Texas," *Texas State Historical Association Quarterly*, July 1911.

———, *Coronado*, Albuquerque, 1949.

BREBNER, J. B., *Explorers in North America*, London, 1933.

CABEZA DE VACA (*see* Núñez Cabeza de Vaca.)

CASTAÑEDA, PEDRO DE, "Narrative of the Expedition of Coronado." In Winship (q.v.).

CHARD, C. S., *New World Migration Routes*, College, Alaska, 1958.

COLTON, HAROLD S., "Prehistoric Trade in the Southwest," *Scientific Monthly*, August 1941.

COON, CARLETON S., *The Story of Man*, New York, 1962.

CORONADO, FRANCISCO VÁSQUEZ DE, "Letter to Viceroy Mendoza, August 3, 1540." Translation in Winship (q.v.).

———, "Letter to the King of Spain, October 20, 1541." Translation in Winship (q.v.).

Selected Bibliography [223]

Selected Bibliography [223]

CORONADO EXPEDITION, *Relacio Postrera de Sibola*, Anonymous. Translation in Winship (q.v.).

——, *Relacio del Suceso*, Anonymous. Translation in Winship (q.v.).

——, *Translado de Las Nuevas*, Anonymous. Translation in Winship (q.v.).

DALE, EDWARD E., *The Indians of the Southwest*, Norman, 1949.

DAVIS, W. H. H., *The Spanish Conquest of New Mexico*, New York, 1869.

DENNIS, T. S., and MRS. T. S. DENNIS (editors), *Life of F. M. Buckelew, The Indian Captive, as Related by Himself*, Bandera, Texas, 1925.

DRIVER, HAROLD E., *Indians of North America*, Chicago, 1961.

——, and William C. Massey, *Comparative Studies of North American Indians*, Philadelphia, 1957.

DUNN, WILLIAM E., "Spanish Reaction Against the French Advance Toward New Mexico 1717–1727," *Mississippi Valley Historical Review*, Vol. II (1915–16), No. 3.

FORBES, JACK D., *Apache, Navajo and Spaniard*, Norman, 1960.

FRAZER, ROBERT W., *Forts of the West*, Norman, 1965.

GOODWIN, GRENVILLE, *The Social Organization of the Western Apache*, Tucson, 1942. Reprinted 1969.

GREGG, JOSIAH, *Commerce on the Prairies*, New York, 1844. Reprinted by Norman, 1954.

HACKETT, CHARLES WILSON, *The Revolt of the Pueblo Indians of New Mexico and Otermin's Attempted Reconquest, 1680–1682, Albuquerque, 1942*.

—— (editor and translator), *Historical Documents Relating to New Mexico, Nueva Vizcaya, and Approaches Thereto, to 1773*, Washington, 1923.

HALL, EDWARD TWITCHELL, JR., "Recent Clues to Athapascan Prehistory in the Southwest," *American Anthropologist*, Vol. XLVI, No. 1, Menasha, Wisconsin, 1944.

HALLENBECK, CLEVE, *Journey and Route of Cabeza de Vaca*, Glendale, California, 1940.

HAMMOND, GEORGE P. and AGAPITO REY, *Don Juan De Oñate, Colonizer of New Mexico, 1595–1638*, 2 vols., Albuquerque, 1953.

———, *The Narratives of the Coronado Expedition*, Albuquerque, 1940.

———, *The Rediscovery of New Mexico*, Albuquerque, 1966.

——— (editors and translators), *Obregon's History of Sixteenth-Century Explorations in Western America*, Los Angeles, 1928.

HARRINGTON, JOHN P., *Southern Peripheral Athapaskawan Origins, Divisions, and Migrations*, Smithsonian Miscellaneous Collections, Vol. C., Washington,. 1940.

———, *On Phonetic and Lexic Resemblances Between Kiowan and Tanoan*, Archeological Institute of America, Washington, 1910.

HODGE, FREDERICK W. (editor), *Handbook of American Indians North of Mexico*, Bulletin 30, Bureau of American Ethnology, Washington, 1906.

———, and Theodore H. Lewis (editors), *Spanish Explorers in in the Southern United States*, New York, 1907.

HOIJER, HARRY, "Southern Athapaskan Languages," *American Anthropologist*, New Series, Vol. XL (1938).

HOOTON, E. A., *Indians of Pecos Pueblo*, Phillips Academy, New Haven, 1930.

HOPKINS, DAVID M. (editor), *The Bering Land Bridge*, Stanford, 1967.

HORGAN, PAUL, *Great River: The Rio Grande in North American History*, New York, 1954.

HULL, DOROTHY, *Castaño de Sosa's Expedition to New Mexico*, Santa Fe, 1916.

HYDE, GEORGE E., *The Pawnee Indians*, Denver, 1951.

———, *Indians of the High Plains*, Norman, 1959.

JARAMILLO, JUAN, "Account Given by Captain Juan Jaramillo of the Journey Which He Made to the New Country, on Which Francisco Vásquez Coronado Was the General." Translation in Winship (q.v.).

JOSEPHY, ALVIN M., JR., *The Indian Heritage of America*, New York, 1968.

KELEHER, WILLIAM A., *Turmoil in New Mexico*, Santa Fe, 1952.

KIRK, DONALD R., *Wild Edible Plants of the Western United States*, Healdsburgh, California, 1970.

LA HARPE, BERNARD DE, *Journal Historique de L'Établissement de Francais a la Louisiane*, New Orleans, 1831.

LOWIE, ROBERT H., *Indians of the Plains*, American Museum of Natural History, New York, 1954.

LUMIS, CHARLES F., *The Spanish Pioneers*, Chicago, 1893.

———, "Fray Zarate Salmeron's Relation," *Land of Sunshine* Magazine, Vols. XI and XII, Los Angeles, 1897–1898.

——— *The Land of Poco Tiempo*, New York, 1906.

McHUGH, TOM, *The Time of the Buffalo*, New York, 1972.

MADARIAGA, SALVADOR DE, *Rise of the Spanish American Empire*, London, 1947.

MANGELSDORF, P. C. and C. EARLE SMITH, JR., *New Archeological Evidence on Evolution in Maize*, Cambridge, 1949.

——— and R. G. Reeves, *The Origin of Corn*, Botanical Museum Leaflets, Vol. 18, Nos. 7–10, Cambridge 1959.

——— and R. G. Reeves, *The Origin of Indian Corn and its Relatives*, College Station, Texas, 1939.

MARGRY, PIERRE, *Découvertes et Établissements de Français dans l'Ouest et dans le Sud de l'Amerique Septentrionale (1614–1754). Memoires et Documents Originaux Recueillis Et Pub. P. Margry*, 6 vols., Paris, 1879–88.

MARTIN, PAUL S., GEORGE I. QUIMBY, and DONALD COLLIER, *Indians Before Columbus*, Chicago, 1947.

MAYHALL, MILDRED, *The Kiowas*, Norman, 1962.

MENDOZA, ANTONIO DE, "Letter to the King of Spain, April 17, 1540." Translation in Winship (q.v.).

MOORHEAD, MAX L., *The Apache Frontier*, Norman, 1968.

NEWCOMB, W. W., JR., *The Indians of Texas*, Austin, 1961.

NÚÑEZ CABEZA DE VACA, ÁLVAR, see Fanny Bandelier, Buckingham, Smith, and John Upton Terrell, 1962.

OPLER, MARVIN K., "The Origins of Comanche and Ute,"

American Anthropologist, Vol. XLV, 1943.

OPLER, MORRIS E., "The Lipan Death Complex and Its Extensions," *Southwestern Journal of Anthropology,* Vol. 1, Austin, 1945.

PACHECO, JOAQUIN F., FRANCISCO DE CARDEÑAS and LUIS TORRES DE MENDOZA (editors), *Coleccion de Documentos,* etc., 42 vols., Madrid 1864–1884.

POWELL, JOHN WESLEY, *Indian Linguistic Families North of Mexico,* Bureau of American Ethnology, 7th Annual Report, Washington, 1891.

RISTER, CARL COKE, *The Southwestern Frontier,* Cleveland, 1926.

ROE, FRANK GILBERT, *The Indian and the Horse,* Norman, 1955.

SCHOLES, FRANCE V., "Church and State in New Mexico," *New Mexico Historical Review,* Albuquerque, 1936.

———, "The Supply Service of the New Mexico Missions in the Seventeenth Century," *New Mexico Historical Review,* Albuquerque, 1930.

———, "Civil Government and Society in New Mexico in the Seventeenth Century," *New Mexico Historical Review,* Albuquerque, 1935.

———, The First Decade of the Inquisition in New Mexico," *New Mexico Historical Review,* Albuquerque, 1935-A.

SECOY, FRANK R., *Changing Military Patterns on the Great Plains,* Locust Valley, N. Y., 1953.

SMITH, BUCKINGHAM, Relation of Álvar Núñez Cabeza de Vaca. Translated from the 1555 edition, Washington, 1851.

SPRAGUE, MARSHALL, *The Great Gates,* Boston, 1964.

SWANTON, JOHN R., *The Indian Tribes of North America,* Bureau of American Ethnology, Bulletin 145, Washington, 1952.

TERRELL, JOHN UPTON, *Journey into Darkness: The Story of Cabeza de Vaca,* New York, 1962.

———, *Traders of the Western Morning: Aboriginal Commerce*

in Pre-Columbian America, Southwest Museum, Los Angeles, 1967.

———, *The Navajo,* New York, 1970.

———, *American Indian Almanac,* New York, 1971.

———, *Apache Chronicle,* New York, 1972.

———, *Pueblos, Gods and Spaniards,* New York, 1973.

THOMAS, ALFRED BARNABY, *The Plains Indians and New Mexico,* Albuquerque, 1940.

———, *Forgotten Frontiers,* Norman, 1932.

———, *After Coronado,* Norman, 1935.

TWITCHELL, RALPH E., *Leading Facts of New Mexico History,* 5 vols., Cedar Rapids, Iowa, 1911–17.

———, *The Spanish Archives of New Mexico,* Cedar Rapids, Iowa, 1914.

UNDERHILL, RUTH, *Red Man's Religion,* University of Chicago, 1965.

WALLACE, ERNEST, and E. ADAMSON HOEBEL, *The Comanches,* Norman, 1952.

WEBB, WALTER PRESCOTT, *The Great Plains,* New York, 1931.

WEDEL, WALDO R., *Prehistoric Man on the Great Plains,* Norman, 1961.

WINSHIP, GEORGE PARKER (translator), *The Narrative of the Expedition of Coronado by Castañeda and Other Related Documents,* Bureau of American Ethnology, 14th annual Report, Washington, 1896.

WORMINGTON, H. M., *Ancient Man in North America,* Denver Museum of Natural History, Denver, 1951.

ZARATE SALMERON, GERONIMO DE, *Relacion (see* Lummis).

Index

Plains Apache is abbreviated PA throughout the index

Oñate, Don Juan de (con't.)
  northern passage and, 99
  PA horses and, 98
ornaments, 42, 120–121
  animal skin, 35
  bone, 35
  as bridal gifts, 214*n*
  from buffalo, 34
  coral, 42
  shell, 35, 42, 110, 120
  tin crosses, 175
Osage, 18, 82, 103, 198
Oto:
  La Salle and, 13
  PA raids against, 13, 14, 18
  PA trade with, 18
  peace with Padouca and, 182–183
  raids against PA of, 55
  as slave traders, 179, 183

Padouca:
  and agriculture, 180
  battle tactics of, 13–14
  described, 18
  destruction of, 184, 185
  French peace treaty and, 182–183
  Kiowa and, 184
  Name of, recorded by La Salle, 13, 18
  need for firearms of, 179–180
  Oñate and, 102, 107
  Pawnee raids against, 180–181, 184
  raids of, against Caddoans, 136
  range of, 15, 180
  as slaves, 179, 180, 183
Paloma:
  Comanche and, 162
  described, 21
  destruction of, 187, 189
  dispersal of, 186
  escape to pueblos of, 187
  Spanish abandonment of, 174
  Valverde and, 162–163
Panateka, 18

Pawnee:
  Black, 181
  cannibalism and, 181
  French alliance and, 162–163, 164, 169, 172
  French gun trade and, 136, 146, 147, 148
  Jumano alliance and, 162–163
  Navejo and, 137–138
  PA raids against, 14, 18
  PA-Spanish alliance and, 147
  PA trade with, 18
  peace with Padouca and, 182–183
  raids of, against PA, 151
  raids of, against Padouca, 180, 184
  Skidi, 179
  as slaves, 137, 170
  as slave traders, 179, 183
  Villasur attacked by, 171
  Villasur emissary and, 170
  Villasur pursuit of, 168–169
Pecos Pueblo (Cicuyé), 155, 187, 189, 219*n*
  Bonilla-Humana Expedition at, 81
  Castano and, 77–78
  Comanches and, 175, 188, 219*n*
  Coronado and, 46
  Faraon and, 22
  Hurtado Expedition and, 153
  Indian governor of, 155
  location of, 45
  minister at, 159
  PA refugees and 187–189
  trade of, with PA, 41, 120, 122, 126
Penxaye:
  described, 21
  dispersal of, 186
  Jicarilla and, 187
  Ulibarri and, 141
  Valverde and, 159
Perillo, 22
Pharaones/Pharoahs, *see* Faraon